The Acts of The Apostles

PROCLAIMING THE NEW TESTAMENT

The Acts
of the Apostles

by
Ralph G. Turnbull

BAKER BOOK HOUSE
Grand Rapids 6, Michigan

Library of Congress Catalog Card Number: 61-10001

First printing, February 1961
Second printing, June 1969

PHOTOLITHOPRINTED BY CUSHING - MALLOY, INC.
ANN ARBOR, MICHIGAN, UNITED STATES OF AMERICA
1 9 6 9

DEDICATED

to

JAMES C. YOUNG

Newcastle, England
Christian layman and leader
a Barnabas encouraging
the preacher

Editor's Foreword

In the series, Proclaiming the New Testament, an attempt is made to provide homiletical comments and ideas. The busy pastor needs to spend time in meditation if he is to offer the bread of life to his people. One of the best known methods of Bible study is to work through one book of the Bible at a time. This gives depth as well as breadth. It provides for the preaching of the whole counsel of God and not just a part of that revelation. As truth must reach people in various stages of growth and at different levels of reception, so there must be variety of communication.

The intention of this series is to stimulate men in the ministry to more definite study. Believing that the first rule of homiletics is to read and study the actual text of Scripture, this method brings ideas and suggestion. Here illustrations are limited as the individual should find his own as he reads or mingles with people, and as he is open to all the winds of God. No pastor can lead his people to a level of thought and spiritual experience higher than the one he occupies. God will not honor lazy men or men who imagine the Holy Spirit should prompt alone. God has given us a mind to use, a heart to love, a spirit to pray, and a will to study.

These results are possible from this approach. *One,* the pastor and student will find suggestive ideas. As Charles H. Spurgeon said of William Gurnall (1616-79), a Puritan, "I have found his work the best thought-breeder in all our library. I should think more discourses have been suggested by it than by any other. I have often resorted to it when my own fire has been burning low. . . ." *Two,* the user will see how to study an entire book of the Bible for preaching values. *Three,* the man of God will be encouraged to begin the study of the Bible book for himself and find by this method other treasures of homiletical insight.

While using the King James or Authorized Version, the student should compare with all other versions and translations as well as the original text when available.

Many and varied are the commentaries available for the profit of the preacher. These include the following:

I. *Critical.* This deals with the text in the light of biblical criticism, seeking to apply historical principles and a rational approach to the text, e.g., *The International Critical Commentary, The Moffatt New Testament Commentary, The Expositor's Greek Testament,* and the commentaries of H. A. W. Meyer, and Keil and Delitsch.

II. *Exegetical.* This seeks to lead out the exact meaning of the text in terms of the words and idioms in the light of their background and use originally, e.g., *The Westminster Commentaries, The New International Commentary on the New Testament, The Evangelical Commentary on the New Testament,* and the commentaries of R. C. H. Lenski, J. P. Lange, and W. Hendriksen.

III. *Expository.* This expounds and applies the dominant theme of each section or unit in the light of history and with relevance to the present, e.g., *The Expositor's Bible, The Interpreter's Bible, Calvin's Commentaries, The Pulpit Commentary,* and *An American Commentary on the New Testament.*

IV. *Devotional.* This brings out the inner sense or the spiritual essence as applied to the soul in meditation. Here is the stimulus to the spiritual life of the believer, e.g., *A Devotional Commentary,* and Matthew Henry's *Commentary on the Whole Bible.*

The present type of book is neither a Bible study book nor a book of outlines. It is not a commentary as the above. We seek to encourage the preacher to engage in the reading and studying of the book to find the homiletical units. As "the servant of the Word" let him work toward this ideal:

the Historical setting,
the Expository meaning,
the Doctrinal value,
the Practical aim,
the Homiletical form

The First Presbyterian Church
of Seattle, Washington

Ralph G. Turnbull
General Editor

Introduction

To expound and interpret The Book of Acts is to attempt an all absorbing task. No book of the New Testament is more appealing as it beckons the church of today to look at the church as it was at the beginning. From the first century we trace how Christ the Lord encountered the world through his church to conquer people with his gospel.

Many and varied are the commentaries which have been written upon *The Acts*. In them are discussions of text, language, background, authorship, criticism, and the problems which arise when questions are asked by inquiring minds. The standard commentaries give help for those who seek such studies and explanation. The present homiletical work is not a commentary. It provides a method of exegesis and exposition leading to the proclamation of the message. This message is relevant for the present age and can be preached with application to our life.

Briefly, the following factors are presented for those who do not have convenient access to the commentaries:

I. IMPORTANCE OF THE BOOK
A. For knowledge of the early Apostolic period of Christianity.
B. A link between the Gospels and the Epistles.
C. An aid to understand the letters of Paul.
D. Explains how Christianity displaced Judaism.
E. Helps to know the Apostolic teaching and creed.
F. Rich biographical and historical value.
G. Missionary methods and the founding and message of the church.

II. AUTHOR
A. Historian—cf. 1:1-4. Same writer of Luke's Gospel.
B. Physician—cf. Col. 4:14. Medical knowledge in the book.
C. Companion—of Paul—cf. II Tim. 4:11; Philem. 24.

III. SOURCES

A. Eye-witness—cf. "We" sections. 16:1-17; 20:5-15.

B. Paul's own notes; speeches; events; a diary kept (?).

C. Paul's letters (although Acts independently written).

D. Help of Barnabas, Philip (21:8), Cornelius (10:1), Mark (Col. 4:10). Various—cf. 1:1-4 and prologue of the gospel.

IV. DATE

Probably A.D. 63. With Paul in Rome and before his release. No mention of the Fall of Jerusalem, therefore before A.D. 70.

V. PURPOSE

A. Not the acts of the apostles really.

B. Not a history of all that is early Christianity.

C. A sketch or selection of events to show the progress of the Faith through the advance of the church.

Cf. 1:1. "began to do ... continued."

"The acts of the risen Lord by the Holy Spirit through the disciples."

VI. KEY

Acts 1:8 suggests the outline of the divine program.

VII. ANALYSIS AND INTRODUCTION

A. The Church in Jerusalem—Jewish witness—Education. Acts 1—7.

B. The Church in Palestine—Transition—Extension. Acts 8—12.

C. The Church in the World—Gentile witness—Evangelism. Acts 13—28.

By the Prologue, 1:1-4, two things are intended:

(a) to convince the disciples of the certainty of the resurrection of Christ because Christianity stands or falls by this event;

(b) to instruct the disciples concerning the Kingdom of God, cf. Acts 1:3, 6, 7.

In *The Acts* we trace "the regularity of the irregular."

The book can be read at a sitting in about two and one half hours. It is thrilling narrative, striking characterization, and dynamic achievement.

Ralph G. Turnbull

Contents

Acts 1

THE WORK OF THE CHURCH

1:8. "Ye shall receive power, after that the Holy Spirit is come upon you; and ye shall be witnesses unto me both in Jerusalem, and in all Judea, and in Samaria, and unto the uttermost part of the earth."

I. HISTORICAL SETTING. This is part of the Introduction to the Book of The Acts of the Apostles. The writer, Doctor Luke, has already written the Gospel which now bears his name. *The Acts* is a continuation of Jesus' ministry in the power of the Holy Spirit. The disciples waited at Jesus' command for forty days until Pentecost for the enduement of power in which they continued His work in the church.

II. EXPOSITORY MEANING. Note the word "power" in Greek. Here is *dunamis* or dynamic power, not *exousia* or authority. "The Holy Spirit" introduces the sweep of the book as the "acts of the risen Lord through the Holy Spirit." The doctrine of the Spirit is vital. "Witnesses" refers to being a *martyr,* one who testifies to the truth. The places named indicate the outreach of the gospel, from the center to the ends of the earth.

III. DOCTRINAL VALUE. The major doctrine is that of the Holy Spirit. Study the references to the divine revelation of the Spirit and His activity in this book. Note the ministry exercised according to the special terms used, e.g., baptism, filling, poured out, gift, received, etc. Other doctrines include that of conversion, the church, and the missionary concern for the whole world.

IV. PRACTICAL AIM. To bring to the individual Christian the strength to be a witness. Testimony to Christ cannot be made in human power. It requires divine enduement. What does this power do for us? What quality of life results?

11

V. HOMILETICAL FORM

Theme: "The Work of the Church."

Introduction: Between the forty days of the resurrection and the ascension, the disciples of Christ were told to await the coming of the Holy Spirit before beginning their life task. They were commissioned by the Lord and appointed to their ministry. The plan and the purpose revealed that the Lord knew He would operate through selected individuals, through special areas of the world, and through promised power.

A. *The Subject of Witnessing* — "Ye shall be witnesses unto me." Throughout The Acts this is the emphasis. The person of Christ is central. The message of the Christian gospel is found here. Christ is the heart of the good news for a non-Christian world. The individual must encounter the living Christ. When the church dilutes her message or compromises with her commission, she neglects Christ at her peril.

B. *The Sphere of Witnessing* — "in Jerusalem, Judea, Samaria, and unto the uttermost part of the earth."

A map will give us the sweep of this directive. In the first century the whole Roman world was in view. Today we think in terms of the entire world as we now know it. The extension of Christianity can be traced as the witnessing went on in every century and throughout all lands. Are there any areas left still to be evangelized? Trace the ever widening circles of influence. This policy is always valid as a principle of universal application. From the Jerusalem center the church moves out to the global. The Acts illustrates this practically, (a) the church in Jerusalem, Chapters 1:7; (b) the church in Judea and Samaria, Chapters 8-9; (c) the church in the Roman world, Chapters 10-28.

C. *The Secret of Witnessing* — "Ye shall receive power, the Holy Spirit coming upon you."

Our Lord promised this. There were some things the disciples could not know (1:7) but the one thing they could know was the experience of power. The Holy Spirit is the promised power. Equipment for service came in this endue-ment. This was *dynamic* energy and was "the promise of the Father" (1:4). Our age knows much about atomic power, the energy in nature which transcends man's powers. That energy unseen has always been present in the universe, but not harnessed until our day. So it was with the disciples as they waited in the Upper Room. The power was there but they did not enter into its benefits until the appointed day of disclosure. Up to that time they were limited in knowledge, but now they would experience unlimited strength for their task.

The Acts is the record of the acts of the Holy Spirit through the church. Supernatural strength is furnished by the Holy Spirit's presence within the disciples in obedience to Christ's command to witness. A witness is one who bears testimony. Disciples first, they became witnesses.

Thus the *work of the church* is clearly seen in this text and throughout The Acts. That work is for all Christians. It is for all parts of the world. It is a supernatural work as it involves the Holy Spirit. In the realm of education, in social reform, in political influence the church has been active. *But* the primary task of the church is not in these things directly. The work of the church is to perpetuate the work of Christ, to practice the message of Christ, and to proclaim the good news of Christ. The apostles seized upon the most tragic event in the life of Christ for their best news. In the strength of that risen life, the power of God was poured into the church. Lacking money, social standing, or political influence, the church made its way through storm and opposition, and triumphed. The world of that day was evangelized. The Acts is the record of that transforming experience, and it begins in this text.

Acts 2

THE PERSON OF JESUS CHRIST

2:22. "Jesus of Nazareth, a man approved of God among you by miracles and wonders and signs, which God did by him in the midst of you, as ye yourselves also know:"

2:23. "Him, being delivered by the determinate counsel and foreknowledge of God, ye have taken, and by wicked hands have crucified and slain:"

2:24. "Whom God hath raised up, having loosed the pains of death; because it was not possible that he should be holden of it."

I. HISTORICAL SETTING. Fifty days after Passover came Pentecost. This to the Jews was the Feast of the First Fruits, the time of the wave offering before the Lord. The new harvest was about to be gathered in. What was significant to the agricultural life of the people now became the occasion of a spiritual harvest. God's time had come to harvest souls out of the world field and bring many into the Kingdom of God and into the body of Christ, the church. There had been Christians or disciples before this, but now they were fused together in a unity to constitute the New Testament church. In this group, Peter, as a witness, proclaims the message of the living Christ to the people without.

II. EXPOSITORY MEANING

Acts 2:22. "approved of God." The idea of being designated or appointed. Here God attests the worth and character of Jesus. The reference to "Jesus of Nazareth" includes the silent years when Jesus was being prepared for his life task.

Acts 2:22. "Miracles ... wonders ... signs." These three words are used to denote the graded ideas in what is unusual in power — (1) the event or act, (2) the amazement of people at this incident, and (3) the reason or meaning attributed to this.

Acts 2:23. "Delivered" and "taken." Attention is focused at the point of the mystery, even the death of the Cross, the divine-human encounter of love with sin.

Acts 2:23. "God" and "wicked hands." What a conjunction of ideas! Divine sovereignty and human free will inter-play.

Acts 2:24. "Raised up" emphasizes the basic note in all the proclamation of this book. Resurrection and ascension are joined.

III. DOCTRINAL VALUE. Peter's sermon bears witness to the truth of the supernatural power of God as revealed in the resurrection and the ascension of Christ — Christ exalted, transcendent, sovereign, reigning. In this section and throughout The Acts the emphasis is upon the risen, living, eternal Christ who is presented as *The Lord*.

IV. PRACTICAL AIM. To bring to the conscience conviction of sin in rejecting the Christ. The moral responsibility for Christ's death Peter lays to the charge of his hearers. He calls upon them to repent and obey the gospel. Such preaching pricked the heart and led to salvation (2:40).

V. HOMILETICAL FORM

Theme: "The Person of Jesus Christ."

Introduction: Pentecost was the "great divide of history." In that hour God acted to release spiritual power on a universal scale. Men from all parts of the world heard the words of life in their own tongue. "The great and manifest day" (2:20) was the inaugural of the new age and God's day of salvation. All this was found in the anticipation of the Old Testament. Now in Jesus Christ the new day had come. Thus Peter insists that the center of life and faith is in this person. But what kind of person? "What think ye of Christ?" is still relevant.

A. *The Christ of the Natural* — "Jesus of Nazareth, a man . . . ."

The manhood and the human nature of Jesus was real. The Gospels and now Peter's sermon bear record that this is history. An ancient heresy called Docetism denied the reality of our Lord's humanity. Another heresy called Appolinarianism denied the reality of his human nature. As a true man, Jesus of Nazareth possessed all the essential properties of humanity. Conceived by the Holy Spirit, born of the Virgin Mary, of her substance, He lived man's normal life, with a true body, and a reasonable soul. He was tempted like all men, yet sinned not. Finally, He suffered, and died and was buried.

B. *The Christ of the Supernatural* — "Approved of God . . . by . . . ."

The supra-normal and attendant events indicate that in Christ the power of God was resident fully. He was more than man. He was also the divine Son of God. God approved Him. God set Him apart, marked him off, and gave testimony to His unique status, "The Beloved" and "only begotten Son." God "pointed out" Jesus for all to see. The attendant events of "miracles . . . wonders . . . signs" point to three stages in God's power displayed. These were evidences to men that God was with Jesus. Hebrews 6:5 speaks of "the powers of the age to come." Here is divine manifestation among men. An ancient heresy called Ebionism and another called Arianism denied the reality of His divine nature. Peter testifies to the deity of Christ.

C. *The Christ of Providence* — "Delivered by the determinate counsel and foreknowledge of God . . . ."

Jesus lived in the knowledge of God's will for his life. "To this end was I born, and for this cause came I into the world . . ." (John 18:37). He had a sense of mission and vocation. To that goal God's will brought him. The counsel of God horizoned or set bounds to that climax. Although evil men worked their will against Jesus, God also overruled in His will. The Cross was no accident or afterthought. Thus the truth that God was *in* Christ in this act.

D. *The Christ of the Cross* — "Crucified . . . ."

Neither a Christless cross nor a crossless Christ is here. "Taken . . . wicked hands . . . slain . . ." is the language of the humiliating experience of suffering and dying by crucifixion. Sin wreaks its evil will upon the innocent and sinless. The New

Testament seeks to interpret this fact of Calvary. It calls not for proof but for explanation. The atonement is an interpreted fact in the New Testament.

E. *The Christ of Glory* — "Raised up . . . ."

The resurrection was the crown and glory of that death. The cross is not the end, nor is the burial. Burial spoke of the reality of suffering death and the end of man's life here. But Jesus was not held by death. The "pains" of death speak of pain in travail, but this could be the "bonds" of death indicating that the prison-house and its bars of brass could not contain the Christ. He burst them asunder. Resurrection and ascension are one in the glorious sweep to the throne of God, the place of authority.

The rest of Peter's sermon continues the strain and note of victory. All was prophesied in the prophets who saw the day of God coming. Now it had come in Jesus Christ, God's anointed one, Messiah, and only Saviour of men. Throughout the sermon, and on through The Acts is found the emphasis on the risen Christ. The constant Easter message is the affirmation of a witnessing and confessing church.

Acts 3

AT THE NAME OF JESUS

3:6. "In the name of Jesus Christ . . . rise up and walk."

3:14. "the Holy One and the Just."

3:15. "the Prince of life."

3:16. "And his name, through faith in his name, hath made this man strong . . . yea, the faith which is in him hath given him this perfect soundness in the presence of you all."

I. HISTORICAL SETTING. The introduction of Christianity into the world brought a challenge to all needs of man. At the beginning there were acts of compassion and love. Miracles were performed in the name and by the power of Jesus Christ. After Pentecost the first fruits were gathered in. The early church began to see the increase as others were brought in. Not only was conversion prevalent, but human needs of the body were also met. The condition of society illustrated by this man who was an outcast has also been described by Matthew Arnold in a picture of the whole of that day,

> On that hard Pagan world, disgust
> And secret loathing fell.
> Deep weariness and sated lust
> Made human life a hell.

The social bankruptcy indicated by the sick man lying at the Gate Beautiful in the area of the temple is a sample of what the church met then and has met in all ages when in touch with human need: socially, physically, and morally.

II. EXPOSITORY MEANING. The context of the story of the miracle brings out certain facts for study. *A map* of the city of Jerusalem should be used to find the temple area and the Gate Beautiful. The temple with its richness and beauty is contrasted with the man in his misery. The Gate Beautiful of beaten brass, in the form of a vine, Grecian made, shone like gold in sunshine. No ailing people passed through (Lev. 21:16-24). No social outcast was welcome. Here is where Christ makes the difference!

"Ninth hour" reminds us of the third hour of the crucifixion, the end of the darkness, the beginning of light. "Going up" speaks of the habit of public worship, the time of prayer.

"Peter and John ... together." Here we have something new — the practical man and the mystic in partnership.

"Silver and gold *have I none;* but such as I have." Here is a contrast of means and supply. Peter does not apologize for poverty, but assesses something greater than gold. Note the interplay of material and spiritual.

"Lame from his mother's womb." Calls our attention to the problem of suffering and handicapped lives. Not all suffering is due to an individual sin.

"Feet and ankle bones received strength" indicates something out of place coming together into socket — articulation of joint. Doctor Luke uses medical terms. The man begins to walk, continues walking, leaps up repeatedly.

III. DOCTRINAL VALUE. An act of compassion, a method of service, and the power of Christ to heal are here. The gift of new life was given to the bankrupt and helpless. The power of the "name which is above every name" is significant. After the miracle comes the message of Peter who interprets what happened. In this the first miracle of the church's history an appeal is made for faith and obedience.

IV. PRACTICAL AIM. To show that social amelioration is not enough. Social reform offered alms or sustenance, but could not change the conditions of disability. Society put up with the outcast man: he could be carried to the gate, but was left outside the temple. Segregation cannot be altered until there is the spiritual dynamic of the gospel to change men's attitudes. This man knew more about ankles and feet than anyone in Jerusalem, but could not walk! Social problems today can be met by new men in Christ.

V. HOMILETICAL FORM
Theme: "At the Name of Jesus."

Introduction: This book is the continuance of the works of Jesus. What he began when among men he now continues as the all-powerful Lord of all life. Absent physically, present spiritually, he is involved in meeting the needs of people through his Spirit in the church. Christ is contemporary in all walks of life. He meets the sinful, the underprivileged, the religious, the educated, the outcast. All classes and conditions find he has the answer for their spiritual and moral welfare. The whole man, physical, mental, social, is renewed. Everything is summed up "in the name." The name is the designation of the person, the expression of the power behind. Thus in this Chapter 3 of The Acts we relate both the *miracle* and the *message*. The former prepares for the latter. The latter explains and interprets what has happened. Thus people are challenged to commitment and salvation of the whole life. All this is gathered up in the names or titles given to Jesus Christ.

A. *The Name that Saves.* 3:6

He who came from Nazareth was known by the name and the title. "Jesus" is his given name; "Christ" is his God-given title. "Jesus the Christ" is probably a better way of expression. He who is God's anointed Saviour is the one we face. Think of all the uses of that name in the New Testament. Jesus means "saviour". (Matt. 1:21). Taken from the Hebrew *Joshua,* the Greek form "Jesus" means that Jehovah is my saviour. He came to save people from their sins. This name given by divine plan predicted the whole life and ministry of God's anointed. He came to lay down his life for the sin of the world. Consider all the hymns we sing about this name: "Jesus, the very thought of Thee . . ."; "Jesus, Saviour, pilot me . . ."; "Jesus, lover of my soul . . ."; "Christ the Lord is risen today . . ."; "At the name of Jesus, every knee shall bow . . . ."

Many passages of the New Testament leap to mind when this name is used. A concordance inspection would surprise us! The Acts itself is full of references wherein the name of Jesus is used in every context of faith and decision. *We pray* in this name; *we sing* in this name; *we worship* in this name; *we give* in this name; and *we serve* in this name.

B. *The Name that Separates.* 3:14 — "The Holy One and the Just."

A surprising element is introduced. While Jesus draws men to himself, he also debars some; he seeks out the lost but he sifts the hypocrite; he saves but he also separates. The sinful may come near to him in repentance, but the unrepentant find they are separated from him. He who is holy and righteous is one who is pure and true. Sin cannot dwell in his presence. Peter cried, "Depart from me, for I am a sinful man, O Lord" (Luke 5:8) — evidence that he felt this awful presence which showed him up for what he really was. The judgment of Christ is a reality and must not be overlooked. We do not deal with a sentimental Christ, but a Christ of holy love and passion. A fire burns to purify dross. The unclean cannot dwell there. Only the pure in heart see God. Those who crucified Jesus preferred a robber to the redeemer, a murderer to the merciful. In denying Jesus they had denied God, and therefore were guilty of heinous sin. Unbelief or disbelief in denial is the final sin. Then is "the magnificant antithesis" according to the German scholar Bengel. Verses 14 and 15 show this truth. Those who asked for a murderer, murdered the Prince of life.

C. *The Name that Pioneers.* 3:15 — "The Prince of life."

The descriptions of Jesus are varied and endless. The Revised Standard Version translates this as "the Author of life"; Moffatt as "the Pioneer of life." Of course Jesus Christ is the author, the originator of life; in him is life, and he has given us life as the Creator and also offers eternal life as Redeemer. However, there is suggestion in the word "pioneer." He is the one who breaks new ground, blazes new trails, explores the unknown. Whether in art, science, geography, medicine, or invention, there is room for the pioneer. Jesus in this thought is the key to all life. He reveals God the Father; he unveils the nature of man; he manifests the love which never lets go; he opened a kingdom to all who believe; and finally, he points to the life beyond. The valley of death and the beyond were mysterious and fearful to men, as the Old Testament spoke little about this. It was our Lord who pulled back the curtain of the eternal a little and gave us a glimpse of the "many resting places" in the Father's house. The "I go to prepare a place for you," and the promises of life and immortality, brought immortality to light through the gospel when he abolished death in his own death and glorious resurrection.

D. *The Name that Completes.* 3:16. "His name, through faith . . . has made strong . . . perfect soundness."

Life is incomplete and unbalanced until Christ takes over. The handicapped man was limited in every way: socially, physically, and spiritually. The whole man was rejuvenated by the power of the name of Christ. The Christian faith brought him into wholeness of life. The imbalance was gone. How true this is when a life is transformed by the power of Christ. The physical miracle here is an illustration of the spiritual miracle when life is transformed. Social problems face the church today. The gospel is social in its expression, touching the individual, the family, and the community. The Christian missionary introduces the school, the hospital, the new agriculture, as well as the church fellowship. It was William Booth and Lord Shaftesbury in England who pioneered social redemption, not socialists or communists, not humanitarians or unbelievers. The evangelical gospel produces the evangelical conscience. The man "made strong . . . with perfect soundness" is the outcome of faith and spiritual redemption. When all parts of a man are coordinated through Christian living by faith, there is a healthy society on the way.

Peter's *message* interpreted the *miracle* as coming from the power of the name of Jesus. The next chapter tells of those who did not like it! Not everyone wishes health of spirit with health of body.

Acts 4

PRAYER AND FELLOWSHIP

4:23. "being let go, they went to their own company."

4:24. "when they heard that, they lifted up their voice to God with one accord."

4:29. "And now, Lord, behold their threatenings: and grant unto thy servants . . . boldness."

4:31. "And when they had prayed, the place was shaken . . . they were all filled with the Holy Spirit . . . they spake the word of God with boldness."

4:32. "And the multitude of them that believed were of one heart and of one soul . . . they had all things common."

I. HISTORICAL SETTING. The previous chapter indicated how a miracle of healing had led Peter to appeal to the people to respond to the name of Christ. The power of this name had operated to effect a miracle of healing. Peter used this to point out the power of God among them. But while some believed and responded, the majority refused to accept this deed as from God. In Chapter 4 the first section deals with this spirit of rejection among the authorities. Peter and John are charged as disturbers of the peace and are threatened with imprisonment. The apostles stood firmly on their conviction of faith (4:19, 20), that what was right in God's sight must be done. The authorities could do nothing with such a spirit, and so let them go.

II. EXPOSITORY MEANING. The association of Christians is stressed throughout this book. In this section is an illustration of that oneness felt by them. They went to their friends — "to their own company." Actually "they came to their *own.*" We are known by the company we keep. "With one accord"

23

indicates the unity of the church. This was "one spirit and passion" in which all shared. Prayer was in unison, and it was unanimous, with one mind. "Boldness" was the courage of the Christian heart. This was expressed in frankness of speech.

III. DOCTRINAL VALUE. Prayer is the vital breath of the Christian. This doctrine is found throughout the book. The only weapon held by the church was the weapon of "all-prayer." Carnal weapons were impossible. The other vital doctrine is fellowship or communion. The *koinonia* (fellowship) is the richest experience of the church — in oneness of faith, sharing life together.

IV. PRACTICAL AIM. To bring courage out of despair and faith out of defeat. In the hour when the church was threatened, the world could have throttled the Christian testimony if the early Christians had lost heart. Persecution did not daunt them. They refused to be quiet even though the authorities demanded their silence. Every age has known this. Today, many around the world are being persecuted, and in America we are easily quiescent because of a false tolerance. We need holy boldness, now, as always, to witness to the Christ. We also need the grace of communal sharing of faith and life which testifies to our oneness in Christ.

V. HOMILETICAL FORM

   Theme: "Prayer and Fellowship in the Church."

   Introduction: The growth of the church in Jerusalem led inevitably to new unfoldings of divine guidance. One lay in the realm of how the church would react when attacked, and the other in how the church would assimilate diverse groups into one body. As a new society in the world new manifestations of personal life would emerge. What were to be the marks of this new life in Christ, and especially within the realm of the many? This is the first recorded gathering for prayer and the first demonstration of brotherhood.

   A. *The First Prayer Meeting. 4:23-31*

   The occasion of this is clear as it resulted from the attack of the enemy from without. Was it not the spontaneous desire of those within? The outward impinged upon the inner. We do not read that the church was praying while the apostles were before the authorities in their trial as they did in Chapter 12:5 later. At this time the church turned to prayer *after* the apostles returned from their trial.

The contrast is drawn of the world attacking Christ's men, and the church replying with a prayer meeting. This would seem foolish to the mind and spirit which threatened. Note the prayer — "Lord, thou art God" (4:24). Taken from Psalm 2, the gist of the Psalm is used in expressing their desires in prayer. Actually, the Lord is spoken of, not only as creator, but as despot (sovereign Lord). The sovereignty of God is affirmed in the prayer, and confidence is expressed in his power to over-rule the affairs of men. Prayer in this conviction is one that is rooted in Scripture wherein God has spoken already. The Psalm is applied as having relevance to the actual situation and the spirit against God is found to be the anti-Christ spirit against God's anointed One.

The spirit of the prayer is not that of vengeance but of vindication. Let men threaten (4:17, 21, 29), but the Christian prays that God would stretch forth his hand *to heal* (4:30). This is ever the response of the church to those who attack her. The gospel brings healing and salvation to men. The church is in a mission to save and not to condemn. Signs and wonders are different words for *miracle,* and these are expected when God works in answer to believing prayer. The church stands still to see the salvation of God in his activity.

The results of prayer are found in the tremors of earth and the tremors of soul. The effect of prayer cannot be measured in physical terms. Possibly when the church was met together they sang Psalm 2, and Peter applied the psalm to the emergency of that hour. The filling of the Holy Spirit implied they were given the spirit of boldness for which they asked. In newly received divine strength they were able to achieve impossible things.

B. *The First Brotherhood.* 4:32-37

The new era of the Spirit manifested itself in this new society of Christians. The common faith led to common ways of life. The spirit of the brethren was shown when they began to share their possessions one with another as a "congregation" (multitude).

The spirit of this communal life (4:32, 33) was rooted in a spiritual experience and not in a material concern. Because they had been baptized into this spiritual oneness in Christ, they were led to this other step. "They had all things common" because they had found a common faith and a community of spiritual life.

The expression of this community life (4:34, 35) was not the communism of Marx and Russia. This was a voluntary giving of self and goods. Nothing was of compulsion. Love not selfishness, was the motive. At the time the act was for a particular situation and to meet a special need. There is no hint that this was to be the standard of the Christian life. In every age groups of Christians have tried this "holy experiment," but not with much success. Individually it still goes on.

The generosity of Barnabas stands out in this context (4:36, 37). Known as "a son of consolation," he acted as the Holy Spirit acted in coming alongside to assist. He brought encouragment and strength to the weak. His voluntary sacrifice of an estate and his gift to the treasury of the church stands out as an example for all time. We shall see later how others gave, but not with the spirit of Barnabas. Such giving as his is the antidote to selfishness, avarice, and covetousness within the church. The question of giving and stewardship is always with the church. How to give? If the spirit of Barnabas caught the imagination of the church, what deeds of sacrifice would be recorded and what victories of the spiritual life would be achieved! We may measure and test our giving in this light.

In retrospect, the early church at this time was a small group to meet the onslaught of the world. The state and society around had no sympathy for the Christians. There was much opposition and persecution. The church learned early to depend upon God through *prayer, fellowship* and *sacrifical giving* to meet the challenge of that day. No better method has been found. Prayer unites the people of God in concert of desire. Fellowship cements diverse factions into one spirit of sharing life together. Giving transforms the vision and outlook of all who share in sacrifice. Thus the pathway of victory was laid out for the church. When we are "in the Spirit," we are led into this fellowship by prayer, and the true unity of Christians is achieved.

Acts 5

THE CHURCH UNDER JUDGMENT

5:1. "But a certain man named Ananias."

5:2. "Kept back part ... and brought a ... part."

5:4. "thou hast not lied unto men, but unto God."

5:3, 9. "to lie to the Holy Spirit ... to tempt the Spirit of the Lord."

5:11. "great fear came upon all the church."

5:13. "Of the rest durst no man join himself to them."

5:14. "And believers were the more added to the Lord."

I. HISTORICAL SETTING. Totalitarian authority in the state had dominated the scene for the early church. Chapter 4 speaks of the threats to the apostles as they tried to witness to Christ. Peter and John were arrested and then let go with threats not to speak in the name of Jesus. Only one thing was left for them to do and that was to do the right in the full knowledge of the consequences from evil men. Christians then and now cannot bow to politics or government or social demands wherein Christ is denied. Bad religion, debased forms of so-called Christianity, and false philosophies are always perils to freedom. This was the setting for the second assault upon the apostles in Chapter 5. In this connection we note also the insidious evil and peril which came not from without but was found within the church.

II. EXPOSITORY MEANING. How illuminating is this section in its detail of the breakdown of professed Christians! Were these people within the ranks of the church but insulated from the power of the Holy Spirit? Had they partaken of Christ by faith? How explain this sudden gust of evil

28

sweeping through the young fellowship in Jerusalem? Human nature is tempted, and human frailty and sin are here unfolded. These people evidently knew about Barnabas and wished to be thought of as on his plane of giving.

Acts 5:1. "A certain man ..." begins the verse and links the previous chapter as all of one story without a break. This shows the contrast of the two men and their actions. What a combination of names and natures — Barnabas, son of consolation or encouragment, and Ananias, hypocrite or liar, the man who acts a part.

Acts 5:2. "Kept back part ... and brought a ... part" points up the kind of Christian profession which is much too common. It is "partial" Christianity. Christ calls for total commitment, not a part! Lying to men seems to be excused in our day of lowered morale. Here lying is seen as sin against God. Lying and tempting the Spirit are twin sins of the spiritual life. Here we grieve and quench the Holy One. "Fear" is not common now, and we wonder why? Is it because the church is not pure?

Acts 5:13-14 indicate that some were restrained from uniting with the church, and others were welcomed when the true spirit was present.

III. DOCTRINAL VALUE. Cheating God or robbing God is never a popular subject among Christians. Malachi, the prophet, speaks of the robbery; but cheating God is similarly condemned. The section points up the demand for absolute honesty with God in money matters, the standards for a disciplined life, and a belief in divine judgment. Judgment begins at the house of God (I Peter 4:17). The vindication of the church before the world is only possible when there is purity. When the church is the church there is power.

IV. PRACTICAL AIM. This should enable the church to clear away all sham and hypocrisy, all too common among us. The test of the success of the church is not in its swollen statistics and gigantic budget or in its social prestige; but the question is, does it have the purity of conviction and life by means of which it makes an impact upon an unbelieving generation? Can it stand up to opposition?

V. HOMILETICAL FORM

Theme: "The Church under Judgment."

Introduction: As this book deals with the living presence of Christ within the church through the Holy Spirit, it is obvious that stress is given to a pure church. The church might be small, insignificant, lacking in many things, but it must be pure. That is not an ideal easily found today. In one sense there is no such thing as a pure church, as no one can read the heart but God. Tares will grow alongside of the wheat. Counterfeits will intrude under cover of Christian profession. Nevertheless, this is pressed — purity.

A. *Hypocrisy Is Unmasked.* 5:1-2

All the enemies, as we have seen, are not on the outside of the church. Ananias and his wife were members of the fellowship. What about the motives which brought on this sin of lying and cheating? Obviously, human nature is the same within the church when it is tempted by avarice and greed. Barnabas had given generously and sacrificially. His spirit was right and it was motivated by love. Now Ananias would emulate him, but with reservation. He would give and endeavor to get the same commendation or credit, but it would not cost him as much as Barnabas. Giving should not be measured alongside of others. We should give *to God.* Motives determine morality. Giving is blessed or marred either by grace or greed. The modern church has many members in the Ananias Club, if church records are any indication of the giving of the members of the churches!

How easily this man spoiled the beauty of his name. Ananias had the meaning of "God is gracious," but now it has become a synonym for "hypocrite." Who would give his son the name of Ananias now? Money is a non-moral commodity, but when used by the Christian it has moral or immoral ends. Values in giving are based upon the spirit and the intention of the giver, not the amount given. Hypocrisy is a terrible thing in the church. The word originally meant an actor, or the man who played many parts. So the debased meaning is now the man of many parts, the liar.

B. *Heinousness of Sin.* 5:3-4

To lie to God or to cheat and rob God is a terrible thing. The offering in the church that day was a pretense. It had all the outward appearance of being sacrificial and therefore a spiritual service in giving (cf. Rom. 12:1), but Ananias blighted it in the sacrilege of pretense. He was not compelled to give. The man who tempts God in this manner tampers with God's portion according to Malachi. "Tithes and offerings" should be taken seriously by the Christian and not passed by as legalistic, or as something to be done or not done according to whims or fancies. Here is where Satan entered into the Christian heart, just as Satan laid hold of and caught Peter (cf. Luke 22:31). No one is safe. Our weak spots are known to the enemy. Is this one of them? Money spells power and many are caught by the corruption of power. Only in stewardship and sacrificial giving are we safe.

C. *Heartbreak of Tragedy.* 5:5-11

This blight of hypocrisy touched more than one life. God's judgment came upon a family, and then upon the whole church. The power and purity of the church then was such that the impure could not remain. It was cast out even as the body of the judged was borne away. Awe and fear came upon the church and also upon the people outside who heard or witnessed these things. The physical judgment of death was matched by Peter's knowledge and insight to know what God was doing. In verse 8, Peter could have pointed to the heap of money lying there from Ananias. Sapphira would see it and know whence it had come. She was partner to the deceit. Sin is personal, but some sins are in partnership, even the family. What about family sins throughout the church? Is it in money matters the family has failed in stewardship? Who decides what is to be given in the Christian family? Is there any guidance by the head of the family concerning proportionate or tithing giving (I Cor. 16:1)? Are the children trained to give of their income also? The Rockefeller family was trained so to give and today are now stewards of millions.

The church of our day is hindered for lack of funds. The income of church people is not low, but usually above the average. Honesty, thrift, diligence, work, reliability — these are associated with the everyday life of the Christian in the world. If every wage earner, every income receiving Christian gave proportionately to God, there would be no lack in the treasury. We multiply luxuries, increase indulgences, yet offerings do not rise very much. Does God *judge* the church? Where is our power? Is it that we lack purity in this realm? Achan in the Old Testament is matched by Ananias in the New Testament.

Conclusion: The verses 12-14 are a commentary and conclusion to this section. The result of God's judgment brought fear upon the people within and without. The church was purified of its dross. The community around was sifted and weighed in the balances. Divine restraint prevented the partially committed person from uniting with the Church. Only those who were totally committed came into the fellowship. Not in numbers, but in selected people was the church enriched for its onward advance through the storm of opposition and persecution. That this is *the church* is indicated in verse 11 where the word *ekklēsia* is used for the first time in The Acts. As such, God's people are seen to be the called out ones constituting the assembly of God.

Acts 6
CHURCH ORDERS

6:1. "in those days."

6:1. "the number of the disciples."

6:2. "the twelve."

6:3. "appoint over this business."

6:4. "prayer, and the ministry of the word."

6:5. "they chose Stephen a man full of faith and of the Holy Spirit."

6:6. "set before ... prayed ... laid ... hands on them."

6:7. "word of God increased ... disciples multiplied."

I. HISTORICAL SETTING. The growth and development of the early church brought its problems of leadership and government. Some today yearn for a church without the organization and overall responsibilities of what seems to be a complicated system. Yet we are shut up to the fact that even at the beginning the church could not remain simply a group of Christians meeting in houses from time to time and nothing else. Because God added believers from outside in society it was inevitable that growth brought problems and needs to be met. New life in the church brought an expanding program of service. Unintentionally the apostles were not giving their full attention to assist the widows under their care. These women were neglected in the daily issue of food and their complaint led to the result outlined in this section. A physical and material situation issued in new spiritual benefits to the whole church.

II. EXPOSITORY MEANING. How striking that this is introduced simply in the words "in those days"! What days?

Those were the days of Chapter 5 with the record of church expansion under persecution. The progress of the church is found in seven summaries (Acts 2:47; 5:14-16; 6:7; 9:31; 12:24; 16:5; 19:20). The judgment of God had vindicated the purity of the church and now came multiplication of the church. Compare "the disciples" with "the twelve." A disciple is a beginner, a learner, a pupil, a scholar, a convert. An apostle was one of the Twelve selected by the Lord to be with him, and then sent forth by him in the missionary work of the church.

Acts 6:3: "This business." How often pious people have discounted the business aspect of the church! This is not secular as over against the so-called spiritual. *Chreia* means "need" or "office." There are things to be done in addition to worship but not at the expense of worship. Worship issues in service. "Prayer and the ministry of the word" sums up the special task of those set apart as apostles. Intercession and exposition go hand in hand.

Acts 6:5. "They chose." Human decisions to select seven men from the congregation were guided by the divine will. Only the qualified and the chosen are of God.

Acts 6:6. "Set before ... prayed ... laid hands on them" indicate the procedure followed in setting apart these men for office and ministry.

Acts 6:7. "Word of God increased and the number of the disciples multiplied" points to the result of obedience to God's will. Converts based upon the Word of God are counted in the divine arithmetic.

III. DOCTRINAL VALUE. Acts 4:33 speaks of "great power ... great grace ..." and now these have operated to produce what is here in Chapter 6. The force of the witness brought the favor of increased conversions. The growth of the church brought out the need to organize. Simple at first, this developed throughout the New Testament program of the church. Even beyond the New Testament the church has continued so to do. Any warrant for the particular organization each Christian communion has, finds its roots here. Is there a progress of doctrine by the Holy Spirit in church order as well as of faith?

IV. PRACTICAL AIM. To show that feeding the needy and caring for the neglected, such as widows and orphans in their affliction is not secular but a spiritual ministry. The church is involved in the affairs of the world. At the first the church gave special note to separate ministries, but each was endorsed by God's blessing and favor. We are truly spiritual when we are practical.

V. HOMILETICAL FORM

Theme: "Church Orders."

Introduction: A reading of Acts 9:41, I Tim. 5:3 and 9-11, 16, provides background for the development of church care for women. The society of the first century had little place for them, especially a widow. The Christian ethic provided for the needy and unfortunate. In this context the church began its *benevolence* program which is now worldwide. CARE is no casual word any longer in this light. It is the church which pioneered to bring relief and succor to the widow, the orphan, the aged, the sick, and the poor. All institutions of healing and care began with this inspiration, long before any government agency took over. Strange that in this practical move a new order and orders for church life and work was born. Consider especially the deacon.

A. *The Selection and Qualifications.* 6:2-5

Instructions were given concerning the manner of election. The church was called together so that this was a democratic procedure (6:2). Consideration of those who might be chosen was then given under the leadership of the Apostles (6:3). "Look out from among you" implied that only those who were within the church would be eligible. Qualifications were important, and later Paul speaks of these in I Timothy 3, when the church had developed further from this initial stage. Note these qualifications:

(1) *Integrity.* When it speaks of "honest report" there is a hint of good repute. Later, Paul speaks of being "grave" and not double-tongued, a man temperate and self-controlled. Money handling, food and drink, social behavior — all these

are important. In order to be qualified, a man must be modest about himself, having Christian conviction, proved and tested for reliability, blameless. If married, the assumed custom of the day, then he must be the husband of one wife, and that wife should not be given to gossip but assist her husband in his service without embarrassment.

(2) *Sagacity*. Wisdom is interpreted in several ways. It implies not only some mental acuteness and understanding, but a common-sense attitude to life. Is this tact in dealing with others who differ? Is it the ability to see another point of view and have an open mind concerning matters of decision? It suggests a business sense: being down to earth; ready to serve in practical ways and meet human needs. Experience is a teacher, and therefore no novice should be appointed.

(3) *Spirituality*. To be "full of the Holy Spirit" is a requirement. The apostle and preacher is expected to be endowed thus, but not always the business man, the steward, the usher, the deacon, the man who serves the church in its temporal affairs. Here the secular has no place in the equipment of the deacon who is to serve. Choice then is not by social standing or prestige, not by wealth, and not exclusively by piety. Spirituality is not to be preferred over the other ideals. There is a trinity of strength in the balanced character who is spiritually minded, ethically and morally strong, and wise in business ability.

B. *The Ordination*. 6:6

After the election by the congregation, the apostles then proceeded to set apart these seven men for their office of deacon or servant of the church. The standard set on this occasion became the practice of the church later (cf. I Tim. 3:8-13). Ordination is something in church order which varies from group to group. Some just recognize their newly appointed officers by the fact that a congregation votes them into office, but no recognition service follows. If it does, then it is marked by a simple declaration of the result of the voting and the men are thus recognized as now holding office. However, there are other communions who take seriously this early apostolic practice of inducting their men into the office before the congregation and requiring of them public confession of their faith and their solemn vows to carry out the duties of the sacred office.

(1) "Set before the apostles." This was the act and choice of the congregation. The people in a democratic manner indicated their choice and believed this to be God's will for them. The apostles were recognized as having leadership because of their special ministry of "prayer and the Word of God." It was the act of the apostles to set these deacons apart.

(2) "When they had prayed." Prayer was important in the ceremony of appointment. Prayer here did not confer any grace but it linked the whole church in the act of ordination through the apostles who represented the whole church. Prayer invoked God to send divine favor upon these men as deacons. Prayer implied that without divine grace and power they would labor in vain.

(3) "They laid their hands on them." In this act was symbolized the fact that under God these deacons were now set apart; they were sanctified unto God and to their new office in the orders of the church. Church Orders are important for the effective mission and ministry of the church. Disorder is not blessed of God. Order is heaven's first law. Laying on of hands did not imply that any grace or power or merit was conferred in any transmitting way. It simply meant that these men were to be recognized by the congregation as having special ministry. What God had chosen they now received.

C. *The Results of good Church Order.* 6:7

God's choice of men having been ratified, the church moved on with increasing power and influence. The Word of God, the truth of the gospel, was spread abroad and many accepted it. New converts, disciples, were added to the fellowship of believers. The church was multiplied and expanded its work, not only in Jerusalem but throughout Palestine. However, it is important to note that in Jerusalem many of the Jewish leaders believed. In the place where Jesus was rejected and crucified, many now turned to belief in His name.

The church by its divinely guided choice gave Spirit-led deacons, and God gave inspiring results of increased membership. Wherever the church is led by dedicated leadership the church moves forward throughout the world.

Acts 6 and 7

A CHRISTIAN MARTYR

6:8. "And Stephen."

6:8. "power ... wonders ... miracles."

6:9. "certain of the synagogue."

6:10. "not able to resist the wisdom and the spirit by which he spake."

6:11. "And we have heard him say."

6:15. "And all ... saw his face."

7:1. "Are these things so?"

7:2. "The God of glory appeared."

7:6. "God spake on this wise."

7:8. "and he gave him the covenant."

7:9. "God was with him."

7:30. "An angel of the Lord in a flame of fire in a bush."

7:32. "I am the God of thy fathers."

7:37. "A prophet ... like unto me."

7:38. "the church in the wilderness."

7:38. "the lively oracles."

7:44. "the tabernacle of witness in the wilderness."

7:48. "the most High dwelleth not in temples made with hands."

7:52, 56, 59. "the Just One ... the Son of man ... Lord Jesus."

I. HISTORICAL SETTING. The church with its newly appointed deacons went on its way to testify to all concerning Jesus the Christ. This led to opposition. Among the Seven Deacons was Stephen. All had Greek names. The Jews who were devoted to the synagogue objected to the new movement because it discredited their inherited tradition and religion. The Christian faith is the flowering of Judaism and the outcome of Hebrew background, but the Jews of that day did not see the relationship of promise and fulfilment in the Messiah, Jesus Christ. Those who did, became disciples: those who did not, remained antagonistic to the church. In this setting Stephen became the spokesman for Christianity.

II. EXPOSITORY MEANING. The section is full of details in which are suggested vital truths. "Stephen" is known as deacon, now evangelist-preacher, and the first martyr of the new church. As a man his character stands out. His message is clear. "Miracle" is described in three ways; as the power exercised; as the wonder of the people who witness; and as a sign from God. "Synagogue" introduces a vital strain in Hebrew life and worship, set over against the Temple worship. *Sunagōgē* — the gathering of people — developed democracy of worship and life. The church later models itself somewhat after the synagogue pattern. "Not able to resist" implies that people find they cannot fight against God and they ultimately recognize the mysterious other power from the unseen.

"We have heard him say." How often hearsay has prevailed! Truth is not always what we think was said. "This Jesus ... shall destroy ... shall change." Prejudice controls the mind and inflames evil action! Distortion of the truth is used as propaganda. Jesus only changed and destroyed to give life more abundantly. "His face" was a sight all saw, reflecting the inner emotion and strength of conviction. What do people see in us? "Are these things so?" This is the dominant question which opens up discussion and debate. Prove what you say and believe. "The God of glory." How majestic is God! Revelation is posited here. God appeared. Man did not find by himself. "God spake." Truth is revealed and God acts in speaking. The Word is normative. "He gave the covenant."

He is the covenant-keeping God in all ages. "God was with him." Divine providence was accepted in a presence. "In a flame of fire." The burning bush is symbol of divine presence and we are not consumed in that holy fire of God's nature. "God of thy fathers." All ages know the same God whom we know. There can be no denial of the past and our spiritual heritage.

"A prophet." Even as Moses, so will Christ be, God's spokesman from God. "Church in the wilderness" — the *ekklesia.* Here the church of the New Testament is linked with that of the Old Testament. That assembly around the tabernacle is forecast of the assembly around Christ who "tented" in this world-wilderness (John 1:14). "The lively oracles" speaks of the eternal word of God written down. *Logia,* alive Scripture revealed by God; made in life, fixed in literature of the Old Testament and New Testament. "Tabernacle of witness." Thus it was a tent of skins tenting for testimony, bearing witness to the truth. Much in the New Testament cannot be understood unless we refer back to this. "Dwelleth not in temples." The universality of God finds acceptance in spiritual worship independent of any place or shrine. "The Just One ... the Son of man ... Lord Jesus." The name above every name has many unfoldings in apprehension by different minds.

III. DOCTRINAL VALUE. The first Christian disputation with those who oppose the church is found here. The proclamation of truth is carried on by preaching and teaching. Witnessing implies the speaking man. Words are necessary. But there is also room for the debate or the apologia, the defense of truth. Recall the Reformation as a later example. Christians defend the truth.

IV. PRACTICAL AIM. All Christian testimony has for its end the conversion of people. This may come first by conviction so that the hearer is convinced he is wrong and the truth commands him. The Holy Spirit's function is to "convict" the world (John 16:9), and here Stephen's address is used to that end. If he spoke in a synagogue and disputed with Saul and others present, he was like a battery fully charged and emitting power (6:10). In 7:51 Stephen becomes passionate in his charge against the enemies of Christ. They are convinced to obey the truth *or* they rebel.

V. HOMILETICAL FORM

Theme: "The First Christian Martyr."

Introduction: The section centers in the life and work of this one man, Stephen. Biographical treatment is best and the outline is clear. We know little about his early life or background, only that he was a Christian. His choice to be a deacon or servant of the church led him into a ministry beyond that of "serving tables." Here was a man who was given gifts of speech and so used them. He is the *layman* witnessing for Christ.

A. *The Man.* 6:8-15

As one of the Seven Deacons set apart by the church, Stephen is given prominence for this one outstanding service. What wonders and miracles he did among the people is not given, but his faith and power are noted. "Faith" here should be *grace* — it was not his faith but the grace of God in his life which was effective.

He was attacked by enemies of the faith, but stood his ground in defense and made his *apologia* or defense of the gospel. He well knew that if his enemies defeated him he stood in danger of being condemned for blasphemy and death by stoning. There were two special charges against him — speaking against the Temple and changing the customs of Moses. He had to plead guilty or not guilty to these charges (7:1). Stephen answered by a historical method.

B. *The Message.* 7:1-53

As we survey this long address we find it is modeled after the usual synagogue address. Two periods of Hebrew history are cited — Patriarchal: (7:1-8) and Israelitish (7:9-50). The value of historical survey cannot be denied. The sweep of the past with its events and message brings truth to the fore. Men learn from the causal events which have produced the changes in men's thinking and actions. Deeds and words are interrelated in history. History is the unfolding of divine providence. Whatever men may see in the events of the past ages, the Christian traces the hand of God and sees the divine care and plan working for our good. God is sovereign and that sovereignty is unchanged.

In this masterful exposition of the Scriptures Stephen defended himself and his faith against those who attacked the church. By a resumé of history he called attention to God's dealings with Israel in preparation for the Messiah. Not that all who listened understood or saw clearly the drift of his words. He began by refuting the charge of blasphemy (7:2) as he confessed his faith in the God of glory, the God of Abraham, the God of the covenant, the God of Moses. The overruling of God is seen in the affairs of the Hebrew people who again and again were not true to their covenant and disloyal to their God.

C. *The Martyr.* 5:54-60

The application of the message was made by Stephen in unmistakable words. They cut to the quick, like a saw rasping the bone. His auditors snarled back at him like a pack of wolves showing their fangs.

Stephen's devotion is definite in that hour of crisis. He does not waver. Threats do not intimidate him.

He was granted the vision of the Christ at the right hand of God. That sovereignty sustained him under the stones. His death by stoning had its repercussions. Those who saw included Saul of Tarsus, who was implicated although he may not have thrown a stone. This was the beginning of the long days of conviction leading to Saul's conversion.

To be a martyr meant to be a witness. We have changed the idea of martyr to mean one who suffers death for a cause. At first, however, it was not so. Then a man died because he was a martyr (witness). He was not a martyr because he died. Here is the link with Acts 1:8 wherein Jesus sent his men forth to be "witnesses-martyrs." Stones do not silence truth. Persecution does not wipe out faith. Death does not destroy the witness. The sacrifice of Stephen will lead to the salvation of Saul. "The blood of the martyrs is the seed of the church" (Tertullian).

Acts 8 (1)

A WITNESSING CHURCH

8:1. "great persecution against the church."

8:1. "they were all scattered abroad."

8:1. "except the apostles."

8:2. "made great lamentation over him."

8:3. "made havoc of the church."

8:4. "they that were scattered abroad went ... preaching the word."

8:5, 25, 26. "Philip went ... to the city ... many villages ... desert."

8:5. "Philip ... preached Christ unto them."

8:9, 13, 19, 21, 22. "some great one ... believed also ... was baptized ... Give me also this power [of the Holy Spirit] ... heart is not right ... Repent."

8:12. "Philip preaching ... the kingdom of God, and the name of Jesus Christ."

8:14, 17. "received the word of God ... received the Holy Spirit."

I. HISTORICAL SETTING. "A religion without the instinct to express itself proceeds not from God." The early church did not depend upon its leaders or the apostles to be witnesses to Christ. All the members seemed to be imbued with the spirit of evangelism. There were local circumstances, however, which aided in this drive. The enemy attacked again by persecution and this led out the church to new fields of endeavor. They were driven out of Jerusalem to Samaria and

44

other parts. Thus the commmission of Acts 1:8 was carried out under divine sovereignty.

II. EXPOSITORY MEANING. The last verse of Chapter 7 is ominous. "Saul consenting to the death of Stephen" sums up the spirit of anti-Christ then prevalent. Then comes the word about the persecution of the church. The "great persecution" was not a passing incident, but a calculated and deliberate attempt to wipe out the infant church by the enemy. "Against the church" has in it the spirit "against the Lord, and against his Anointed" (Ps. 2:2), which Saul himself was to discover later when he was converted (Acts 9:5). The fight against the church was really the fight against Christ. "Scattered abroad." The whole church was disrupted and spread out over the land. Hitherto, the Church had been chiefly in Jerusalem, but now it was diffused. "All" the members "except the apostles," indicates how God would have every member evangelize. No professional group or class did this work. The divine strategy of missions is here.

They "went . . . preaching the word" indicates how God uses circumstances to work out His purpose of worldwide missions. The word is the seed to bring the harvest. Sown earlier by Jesus at Sychar, it would be reaped soon. "Lamentation over him [Stephen] . . . made havoc of the church" stresses the terrible nature of evil deeds. When the church sorrows and mourns, then the enemy increases attacks. How often has the church seemed to be blotted out, yet has endured. "City . . . villages . . . desert" speaks of evangelism in different spheres, but it is the same message. "Philip preached Christ." Note the linking of preaching Christ and preaching the kingdom of God. Are these the same? What elements are different? Philip *ekērussen* as a herald the person of Christ, but he *euaggelizomen* as an evangelist the things of the kingdom. "Some great one." This man who entered the church and was baptized was not right in heart. The church cannot be sure that everyone is truly Christ's. "Received the Word . . . received the Holy Spirit." These are equally important. One without the other incomplete for total Christian experience. The Spirit illumines the Word.

III. DOCTRINAL VALUE. God uses circumstances to work out His plan and purpose for the church. Divine providence is seen in the over-ruling of Stephen's martyrdom and the persecution of the church. Men plan against God, but God overturns their attempts and in sovereign grace works on behalf of His own. The triumphs of the gospel are indicative of what had been done. God uses men like Stephen and Philip, but he also uses the unknown members of the church when they scatter the seed of the word of God.

IV. PRACTICAL AIM. To show that the whole church and not only Stephen is a "martyr" — a witness. This is a martyr church, a witnessing body. Then this shows how the gospel must be given to the whole world and not limited to the place where we are. And then we see how God overrules evil with good. Tragedy is made to serve God's providence. Stephen is taken, but Saul will come. The church will be scattered, but the gospel will be scattered throughout the entire world.

V. HOMILETICAL FORM
    Theme: "A Witnessing Church."
    Introduction: World conditions today raise the question about the suffering and martyrdom of Christians. In many lands we are seeing a resurgence of the spirit of evil attacking the church. This is true of the younger churches of Christendom, especially in the Congo, South America, China, and under Russian Communism. The Acts is relevant for its light upon the experience of early Christians in their ordeal of suffering. Whatever the outcome, the church must be known and seen as a witnessing people. The Christian testifies that Christ is Saviour and the Lord of Life. There can be no compromise with this message. The enemy will reject this and oppose, but Christians must stand and take the consequences, knowing that the seed will bring the harvest in God's time.
    A. *The First Mission* — Evangelism by the Church. 8:1-8
    The persecution at Jerusalem drove the Christians out into the hinterland of Palestine (8:1-4). Samaria was next in receiving the gospel. In this neglected area Philip, the deacon and evangelist, reaped where his Master had sown earlier (John 4:35), and where also the outcast women had sown seed.

"And the multitudes gave heed with one accord, unto the things that were spoken by Philip" (8:6). "And there was much joy in that city" (8:8).

When this took place there was nothing of modern ways of publicity; no committees of welcome; no cordial reception by leading people; and certainly nothing but turbulence and trial. The *conditions* were not conducive to evangelism — or were they? Stony ground can be broken up; thorny ground can be cleaned up: and any kind of soil can become fruitful for the divine seed. Picture the scene in Jerusalem as Saul and others went from house to house to devastate the Christians — as they met in homes — just when these Christians were in danger of staying too long in that city and forgetting to carry out the commission of the Lord. Did they tarry too long?

The *field* for evangelism is indicated (8:5, 25, 26). Later we shall see Philip reaching a solitary man on a desert highway. Here we see the thrust of the gospel in city and in villages. Divine strategy would include both. Philip — not the apostle — deacon and evangelist carries the message of salvation. He is also known as a teacher (21:8). Here he is the herald *(ekērussen)* of Christ; and the teller of good news *(lalēsantes)* concerning the things of the kingdom of God. What did he interpret this to be?

The Samaritans were a people despised by the Jews. Racial and religious differences created prejudice. From II Kings 17 we learn of the capture of Israel, the northern kingdom of the Jewish people, about 722 B.C. When taken to captivity, Assyria brought in other captive peoples to settle in the land and thus Samaria became a "mixed" people, partly Hebrew and partly Gentile. To evangelize this people was a most difficult task for a Jew now a Christian, knowing well the traditional hatred and dislike of one people for another. However, this is exactly the work of the gospel and the evangelist — to bring reconciliation "in Christ" to all.

The response (8:6-8) was noteworthy. This was harvesting as well as sowing. Not everyone is given this joy. Philip learned that his Master had been ahead of him. The spirit and interest of the people is marked as they responded to the gospel. Unless people "give heed" it is most difficult to win them. Here were people ready, eager, waiting for the opportunity. We need never hesitate to go to the unknown people around us — they may be ready and prepared by God for our coming. We should aim to reach the unlikely, the unlovely, the forgotten, and those who seem to be antagonistic. The church must evangelize city and village.

B. *Tares Among The Wheat.* 8:9-24

The heretic or counterfeit is unmasked. Among those who professed faith in Christ was Simon, a sorcerer. His background was a religion of magic and superstition by which he exploited people for money. He gulled or bewitched people. This is nothing out of date. Our day knows much of similar exploitation by "religious" teachers and founders of cults who get rich thereby.

(1) His Profession (8:9-13). Simon lived in the glare of publicity as "a great one." Impressed by the power of God as seen through Philip, Simon thought he saw a chance to make more money. He thought he could *buy* the power of God! Was his profession of faith in Christ genuine before he came to this fatal step? Or was he merely a surface-believer, having the attitude that all religions were alike and believing that to embrace the Christian faith would give him another label for leverage in his ill-gotten gains from credulous people?

(2) His Error (8:14-19). Simon's sin is that of *simony*. Unscrupulous people do enter the church under guise of profession. There are those who trade upon the weakness and credulity of the ignorant and spiritually unenlightened. The sin of simony has plagued Christianity in every age. The gospel of grace is without money and price for salvation and we rightly suspect those who put a price upon their services, whether Protestant or Romanist. When money is allied to "power" we may well beware of all cults, sects, denominations, or religious evangelists or leaders who have their price.

(3) His Condemnation (8:20-24). Divine judgment came upon Simon when Peter and John came to investigate. Christianity is against magic and superstition. Peter and John rep-

resented the church from Jerusalem. Once they had asked the Lord for fire to descend from heaven upon the Samaritans (Luke 9:54) ; but now they are among Samaritans to protect them and to share with them the blessing of the gospel of love. Simon had been baptized by water (8:13) ; but now Holy Spirit baptism and reception was shown to be more important (8:14-17).

The false gives way to the true; the counterfeit to the genuine. Christianity wins its way among prejudiced people, in city and in village, and overcomes superstition and evil.

Acts 8 (2)

EVANGELIZING THE INEVITABLE

8:26. "Arise, and go ... way ... desert."

8:27. "And he arose and went: and behold, a man of Ethiopia."

8:27, 28. "had come to Jerusalem for to worship ... Was returning."

8:28. "read Isaiah the prophet."

8:29. "Go near, and join thyself."

8:30. "Understandest thou what thou readest?"

8:31. "How can I, except some man should guide me?"

8:32. "The place of the Scripture which he read was this."

8:35. "began at the same Scripture, and preached unto him Jesus."

8:36. "what doth hinder me to be baptized?"

8:39. "he went on his way rejoicing."

8:27, 31, 34. "a man ... some man ... some other man."

8:4, 5, 12, 25, 35. "preaching ..." (several variations).

I. HISTORICAL SETTING. The widespread outreach of the gospel throughout Samaria and Palestine was encouraging for the early Church in carrying out its commission to reach the entire world. Philip, the evangelist, was engaged in a fruitful mission in Samaria and in city and in village the response was excellent. In the midst of this, and when he was harvesting from the seed sown, suddenly he was called by the Spirit of God to leave. Why this is so is a mystery of divine

50

unfoldings. Certainly it is a test for the servant of God. To leave the crowd and seeming success is not easy. His ministry in Samaria was doubtless one that built up friendships and the foundation for the church there. He was needed in one way to stay for a while, yet God ordered otherwise. Faith obeys knowing that God's will has its compensation. It is not the place which is important, but the will of God for the life of the servant. To the south there was a man waiting for the evangelist, and beyond that man, a dark continent waiting for the gospel.

II. EXPOSITORY MEANING. There is always a messenger of God to direct and give guidance. Philip was surprised when so directed but went willingly. "Arise and go." "And he arose and went." Obedience is the divine organ of spiritual revelation. Faith rests in the unexplained because God holds the key of all unknown. Philip went to the highway or road on the way to Gaza. On one of the main routes from Palestine to Egypt seemed an unpromising place for evangelism and missionary work! "A man of Ethiopia" was there traveling. His rank and status are set forth in detail. His spiritual need is soon discovered and the need for the evangelist. "To worship . . . Was returning." How often men are disappointed in their search after truth and God. "Read Isaiah" — the evangelical prophet is full of good news. "Join thyself" (*kollētheti*) carries the meaning of to glue or to cement. Evangelism is sticking to one until won for Christ. "Understandest?" Do you know what you think you know (*ginōskeis ha anaginō skeis*)? Man can read without knowing. Reading aloud was the custom then and there were no breaks between words in the old scrolls. The Isaiah scroll would likely be one in the Greek translation of the Old Testament, the Septuagint. "Guide me?" He has need for an interpreter (*hodengēsei*) — someone to read with him. "Place of Scripture." How often a particular passage or text has all we need. "Began . . . same Scripture . . . preached Jesus." This is true for the whole Bible. All Scripture begins and ends with Christ. "Baptized" — visible sign of cleansing and faith. "Rejoicing" is a consistent element in new-born faith (cf. 8:8). "A man . . . some

man . . . some other man" — three in a chariot! One is a
seeker after truth; the second is the evangelist; and the third
is the Saviour. "Preached": (8:4) preach the word *(euaggel-
izomenoi)*, (8:5) preach Christ *(ekērussen)*, (8:12) preach the
kingdom *(euaggelizomenō)*, (8:25) testify and preach *(diamar-
turamenoi* and *lalēsantes)*, (8:35) preach Jesus *(euaggelisato)*.

III. DOCTRINAL VALUE. The church must know its true
mission in the world. We talk about evangelism as though
this were something different from the missionary enterprise.
Then some talk about the church being *in mission*. We might
as well talk about the church being in evangelism or in education. Actually, the Church *has* a mission. We have a work
to do — it is the evangelistic thrust to all people. Whatever
difficulties or seeming success comes to the church, the church
must never lose sight of the individual, whether in the city or
the villages, or the solitary man on the highway. Mass evangelism with its crowds has its place; visitation evangelism from
home to home in the community is important; but finally, all
evangelism is the individual being confronted with Jesus
Christ. Personal evangelism is the task of the church and here
we see Philip at work.

IV. PRACTICAL AIM. When the church is attacked and
persecuted there are times when the true work of the Church
may be neglected because people are thinking of saving their
own lives out of political, social, and warlike conditions which
operate against the church. However, at such a time there is
given an opportunity to spread the gospel through the upheaval and tensions which prevail. Let the attack on the
church come and then others will see how Christians react
to witness to their faith in such a time as that. Then, when
the church is respected and honored in a community, there
is peril because we are in danger of assuming that no one needs
to be evangelized. Toleration and lack of opposition to the
church is no indication that people in the community believe
or accept the church's message. Evangelism is still a "must."

V. HOMILETICAL FORM
  Theme: "Evangelizing the Inevitable."

Introduction: No one can estimate the worth of a single life won for Christ and dedicated to His service. Adoniram Judson left America for India and entered Burma. He went to a barren field and for many years there were no converts, yet the church was established in Burma. His obedience to go to the "desert" was worthwhile. This section relates how Philip obediently left the crowd to go to the uninviting place. Evangelism must undertake to proclaim Christ everywhere and to all people, without distinction. Inevitably every man must be confronted with the gospel.

A. *The First African Convert.* 8:26-28

This man was one of high rank in the government of Ethiopia. The area was not the modern Ethiopia, but south of Egypt generally. As a state official he was treasurer for the Queen whose name, Candace, simply refers to the title of Pharaoh. His religious interest is obvious. He had been to Jerusalem seeking help spiritually. The worship at the Temple; his association as a possible proselyte to Judaism; and his continued search by reading the Scriptures suggest that he was a man of earnest purpose and sincerity. Worship (*proskunēsōn,* a rare word in the New Testament) suggests purpose.

As we think of him reading we understand this to be reading aloud (as was customary). Bible reading is one of God's ways of reaching people. Millions of people own and possess a copy of The Bible. Not all read it. If induced to read there would be a basis of appeal and understanding for the evangelist. Large numbers today are spiritually and Biblically illiterate. This well-educated leader in a nation had some knowledge of the text. His problem was simply that he did not understand. He could not enter in to the spiritual meaning of what he read. Many are like him. That he did not grasp the meaning of verse 32 and its Messianic reference is not surprising. Before Christ's advent and the illumination of the Spirit many Jews did not know that the Suffering Servant of God was the Messiah. They thought of the nation Israel as that servant. Only the New Testament interpretation in the coming of the Spirit's enlightenment brought the whole truth.

B. *The Evangelist's Instructions.* 8:29-35

The zeal of Philip is noted as he eagerly runs alongside of
the chariot and steps up when invited to sit with the Ethio-
pian. Courtesy, tact, and a pleasing spirit are helps in evangelism. We must never intrude into the privacy of the soul.
The approach was by a question — as there Philip heard the
man read aloud and there was no impropriety to ask. He
appealed to the man at the point of contact — the reading
of the scroll.

"To join" himself to the chariot implied that Philip was
bidden by the Spirit to glue himself — make contact and do
not let go of this man until he is won for Christ. That is soul-
winning. Too easily Christians give up their task.

As Philip talked, there was a play upon the words in the
original — "Do you know what you know again [read]?" "Of
whom speaks the prophet?" All Scripture and all evangelism
leads to the person of Christ. He is the key to unlock the
mysteries of life and to open the doors to fulness of life.
Christ was found in and through the Old Testament (cf. Luke
24:27; I Peter 1:11; II Peter 1:19-21).

C. *The Confession of Faith.* 8:36-40

Another man was added to the membership of the church
of Christ. Another witness was prepared to live and speak
for the new faith. Africa received a missionary who came
home with joy. The act of baptism is linked with the Great
Commission and discipleship. In every age the church has
baptized its converts. Various are the interpretations of this
rite, but one thing is clear, that it is linked with Christ and
faith. This is not the only reference to baptism and the subject must be studied in its wider context. In this section we
see it as the natural outcome of faith and obedience on the
part of the convert to Christ. The old has passed: the new
has begun.

Confession of faith comes in many ways. We must leave
the Spirit to guide Christians in these things. The story ends
with Philip being caught away to another area of evangelism,
while the man of Africa goes home, no longer disappointed
but dedicated to Christ and the gospel. Think of all the work

of missions in Africa throughout the centuries and know that this was the initial thrust. It was inevitable that Africa would receive the message.

Acts 9

A RELIGIOUS MAN'S CONVERSION

9:1. "And Saul, yet breathing out threatenings and slaughter."

9:2. "any of this way."

9:4. "Saul, Saul."

9:6. "Lord, what wilt thou have me to do?"

9:2, 8. "bring them bound unto Jerusalem ... led him by the hand and brought him into Damascus."

9:10. "a certain disciple ... named Ananias."

9:11. "the house of Judas."

9:11. "one called Saul ... for, behold, he prayeth."

9:13. "Thy saints."

9:15. "a chosen vessel ... bear my name ... suffer for my name's sake."

9:17. "Brother Saul."

9:19. "when he had received meat, he was strengthened."

9:25. "Let him down by the wall in a basket."

9:26. "They were all afraid of him, and believed not that he was a disciple."

9:27. "But Barnabas took him."

9:31. "Then had the churches rest ... were edified ... walking in the fear of the Lord, and in the comfort of the Holy Spirit, were multiplied."

I. HISTORICAL SETTING. The persecutions which broke out in Jerusalem against the infant church continued after the death of Stephen because the enemy had a leader. Saul of Tarsus, member of the Sanhedrin, a zealous Hebrew, thought it his religious duty to exterminate Christians. Chapter 8:1 began with the fact that Saul sought to devastate the church. Now in chapter 9:1 the story is continued. Although Chapter 8 indicated the victory of the church in its evangelism throughout Samaria, the church was not safe from attacks. It was in this context that the sudden miracle took place in the conversion of "public enemy number one" — Saul. The enemy of Christians is converted to the Christ and comes over to the side of the church to serve the church with all his might.

II. EXPOSITORY MEANING. The details are striking as we see how Saul found a new master and entered upon a new life. "And Saul, yet breathing out." There was no diminution of the attack against Christians by this man. Notwithstanding the evangelism in Samaria, Saul led the onslaught against the church. He seemed to have tasted Stephen's blood like some wild animal, and could not be restrained. Acts 26:11 speaks of him being "mad against them," although later he confesses in I Tim. 1:13, "I did it ignorantly in unbelief," and in Acts 26:9 he claims to have been sincere in what he did in the name of Hebrew religion. Verse 5 of this chapter points out that he was kicking against the goad, and that in conscience he knew he was under divine pressure even though he fought against God. "Of *the Way*." This must be written with a capital W to bring out its deepest meaning. Christian disciples were the people of The Way, even as they followed the new way of life of Him who said, "I Am the Way, the truth and the life" (John 14:6). "Saul, Saul." This double use or repetition of the personal name implies emphasis and a call to the man. Christ had singled him out. "Lord, what wilt thou have me to do?" — the obedience of faith after awakening of new life. Repentance leads to restitution; conversion to consecration; salvation to service. "Bring them bound to Jerusalem . . . brought him to Damascus." What contrasts are here! Everything is turned round. Man's plans are radically altered in the

divine intervention. "Certain disciple . . . Ananias." This one
kept the good name as given and did not stain it like another
Ananias (Acts 5:1-10). "House of Judas" — a Christian home
and center for disciples to gather, with a name redeemed from
that of the traitor who betrayed our Lord. "One called Saul"
— reminding many of another Saul, a king who failed: this
Saul has an opportunity to make good. "He prays." This is the
mark of a new Christian. "Thy saints." This is the *first* time
this is used of God's people, and always in the plural. Saints
live in community and family. Paul is a "chosen vessel" — a
selected instrument of God —to witness and to suffer. "Brother
Saul" —first use of acceptance of another in the church with
its fellowship and belonging one to another, transcending all
barriers. "Meat . . . strengthened" — Christianity neither asceti-
cism nor fanaticism, but balanced life of spiritual and physical
intertwined. "Let down . . . basket." What a contrast for the
proud Pharisee who once sought out Christians to exterminate
them! Now he has to escape for his own life as a Christian in
this embarrassing way. God uses insignificant and small means
for his ends. "Afraid of him." It is no wonder that at first they
did not receive him with his reputation of evil! "But Barnabas" — here the man of consolation and strength is alongside
to encourage and believe in him (as he will John Mark
later even though Paul then will not accept Mark!) Here is
Christian brotherhood when a man is in desperate need. "All
the churches had rest. . . ." This is the summary of progress
after the conversion of Saul.

III. DOCTRINAL MEANING. Conversion is a reality of the
life of man. Not all are alike. There is a variety of Christian
experience. This religious man Saul was not brought to faith
like the Eunich of Chapter 8, or as the business woman Lydia
in Chapter 16. Attending Saul's conversion were the light, the
voice, and the person of Christ, and Saul fell to the ground,
blinded, and then surrendered to Christ. Many are converted
without any visible manifestation or unusual phenomenon.
The light, the voice, the prostration, the blindness — these may
be absent. What matters is that Christ is known and his will
obeyed. At the same time Saul was called also to be an apostle.

The church moves forward in its mission through conversions.
IV. PRACTICAL AIM. To show that conversion is the experience of many. Trace through this book of The Acts the different kinds of people who are converted, whose stories are recorded. Saul's story is given three times (Acts 9, 22, 26), so that this is important. It is vital to study his testimony and the account by Dr. Luke as Saul is the most important character in the New Testament after our Lord. His life and work, his writings and influence, make him pre-eminent in contribution to the church and the world. To understand Paul is to have the best interpreter of Christ beside us.

V. HOMILETICAL FORM

Theme: "A Religious man's Conversion."

Introduction: The background of Saul's life is worth studying. The preaching of Paul later will interpret this experience. That Saul of Tarsus was against Christ at the first is valuable in showing that the pent up tension within his soul was built up through the insistent conscience-voice reminding him of Stephen's death to which he consented. Was there also the fact that when Stephen voiced the words of forgiveness for his enemies, Saul remembered the same words as coming from the Son of God from the cross of Calvary? Was Saul an eye-witness of that crucifixion? What a subject for study — the psychological and spiritual mind of this man in his interior life which led to the crisis hour!

A. *The Conversion.* 9:1-9

He is seen as Persecutor (9:2), and all he did then was against the church. Later, he was to discover that he was fighting against the Christ. He who touches the church attacks the Lord of the church. This wolf will be converted and changed to become a good sheep-dog to guard the sheep and the flock of Christ.

As a Convert (9:3-9) the turning point was in the open air, on the roadway to Damascus. What a scene and what an hour! This was epoch-making in the history of Christianity.

(1) The Vision. Christ is seen and known as the eyes of understanding are enlightened and Saul knows even as he is smitten to the ground.

(2) The Voice. Others heard a sound, but did not know what was said when Jesus talked to Saul. They were conscious of the light but were unaware of the Light of the world. Saul heard in his soul and knew that voice in his heart.

(3) The Vocation. What God wished him to do and to be was all that mattered thereafter. The lordship of Jesus Christ is the whole of Christian experience. Led out of physical blindness Saul is given spiritual illumination later. The new obedience is the expression of the new faith by new life.

B. *The Consecration.* 9:10-19

When Saul was led to Damascus he entered into a new life entirely. The old was shattered. It would take time (possibly three years in Arabia) to find poise and balance, but this one thing was sure; he had found the Messiah-Saviour, and he was now one of the church family.

This section stresses the reality of fellowship wherein Saul is made to become a member of a community. He is baptized; he prays; he is given the right hand of fellowship as a member of the redeemed family; he is called brother; he is now one of the saints; he becomes a chosen vessel of God; (Christ chose or elected Saul before Saul chose Christ) ; he confesses his faith; he partakes of food in fellowship; and he begins to testify and preach that Jesus is the Christ.

C. *The Consequences.* 9:19-31

After confession and commissioning Saul enters upon a new life of service for the new Master. Surprise is everywhere, both among the Christians who seem incredulous and also among the enemies of Christ who are skeptical and disdainful. Yet Saul has to prove to both the reality and sincerity of the changed life. The glory of the lighted mind is now his and he begins to translate his faith into action.

The church — and here there are congregations as part of the whole Church — now has rest for a while. During that period there is growth and progress in spiritual life and in numbers. Thus through the storm of opposition the church has made its way, and Christ has won his enemy to become his slave. This is the perpetual miracle in every age.

Acts 10

A SOLDIER CONVERTED

10:1. "Cornelius, a centurion."

10:34. "God is no respecter of persons."

I. HISTORICAL SETTING. As Christianity moved throughout the world of the first century, the missionaries of the gospel carried the message to all people. At first, the witness centered in the city of Jerusalem; then it moved into Samaria, and finally it reached out to the uttermost parts of the Roman Empire. There were changes in the attitudes of those early leaders who had to find release from the bondage of legalism and Judaism for the sake of the freedom of the gospel. After the conversion of Saul, Peter was led into a new area of commitment when he faced the Roman soldier, Cornelius. Geographically, he had moved also from religious Jerusalem to the busy work-a-day world of the seaport, Joppa. In a new environment and under new conditions, the gospel found its way.

II. EXPOSITORY MEANING. To find out the kind of man who was converted, a review of this chapter is revealing. Peter, of course, occupies a central place as the channel of communication of truth, but the Roman soldier is described in some detail.

Acts 10:1. "A certain man in Caesarea." This city was twenty-eight miles from Joppa (Joppa is the oldest town in Palestine). "Centurion of the Italian band." Cornelius was leader and captain over one hundred legionaries, special detachments from Rome.

Acts 10:2. "Devout . . . feared God . . . gave alms . . . prayed." Here we have indication of a high quality character earnestly seeking for light and truth. Cornelius had been brought up in the Roman Empire with its many religions, yet desired something else to satisfy. He was a truly religious man in the best sense; yet one can be religious and not Christian.

Acts 10:3, 4. "Vision . . . memorial before God." In this response to faith, the prayers of Cornelius had been heard. In 10:2 *deomenos* (prayed) and in 10:4 *proseuchai* (prayers) are united; the one being the act of begging and the other being the acts of memorial. Prayer is a mystery and yet a simple way of contact with God. What was given in "vision" in the insight of spiritual apprehension to the soul, is matched by the "memorial" before God. God remembers what a man offers and does in faith.

Acts 10:5. "Now send to Joppa and call for Peter." Is this not a strange answer to prayer? Was Cornelius expecting God to do something out of the ordinary then? God usually works through the ordinary, the natural, and through ordinary people he has chosen as his agents.

Acts 10:19. "While Peter thought on the vision . . . three men." The prayer of Cornelius to be answered meant that Peter had to be readied and found willing to serve God. Peter also had been given a "vision," and the outcome of it was — "three men calling upon him."

Acts 10:25. "Cornelius . . . fell down . . . worshipped." This indicates the limited knowledge of the Roman soldier. This word is not that of an idolator, but the idea of "reverence." Peter may have taken it to mean the ultimate act of worship which belongs to God alone.

Acts 10:33. "We are all here present before God, to hear all things that are commanded Thee of God." This is the spirit of the soldier — under orders. He is obedient in faith, open in mind, ready to hear what God commands (*prostetagmena*).

Acts 10:34. "God is no respecter of persons" (*prosōpolēptēs*) no respecter of a face! Looks are not as impoₜtant as character. The Jew is known characteristically by his looks, yet Peter learned that God is more concerned with the inner condition than the outward.

Acts 10:35. "Accepted with him." How is a man accepted by God? The word *dikaiosunēs* means that in our true state God is ready to meet us at that point.

Acts 10:36. "The word which God sent." Here is a fine summary of the message of Peter, beginning with the theme of the Lordship of Christ. The whole gospel is summed up in "He is Lord of all." "The *word*" is the good news, the message, the preached truth.

Acts 10:37-43. A Christology is presented here, just as Peter gave a similar one in preaching in Acts 2. All proclaiming of the New Testament message has in it this deposit of truth and revelation. Mark's Gospel in outline is found in germ here. Did John Mark write his Gospel after hearing Peter preach this way again and again?

Acts 10:38. "Jesus . . . went about doing good" — a beautiful description!

Acts 10:44. "The Holy Spirit fell on all . . . which heard." This Cornelius and his family and servants become Christian in obedience to the truth.

III. DOCTRINAL MEANING. The witness to Christ by the early Christian produced a new ferment in the society of the Roman world. Ancient animosities, racial division, religious bigotry, and vested interests were challenged and transformed by the grace of God. Here is the answer to most of the world's ills wherein caste and custom, race and color, language and culture are in tension to divide people. Christ comes to unite the severed and rifted groups and individuals by his message of redeeming love and the atoning sacrifice of the cross. Peter, as the man in the middle, soon found that he could no longer remain a bigot in his insularity and pride of race. The barrier was broken down in the conversion and acceptance of Cornelius into the Christian brotherhood and fellowship.

IV. PRACTICAL AIM. Through this event the whole church was led out to a wider ministry. Hitherto, the church had tended to remain within Palestine and minister largely to Jews, except where Samaria was concerned. Now God leaps over the wall of nationality and race. In the conversion of Cornelius a new day comes and the outreach of the gospel spreads beyond the little land of Palestine to take in the whole Roman Empire. The soldier will become a missionary. The marching legions will carry the gospel as well as their arms. The highways of the empire will become the pathway for the spread of the divine message. The church must never hesitate to speak of Christ to every man without distinction.

V. HOMILETICAL FORM

Theme: "A Soldier Converted."

Introduction: In our modern world we are actually aware of the tensions of war. Our nation as well as other nations maintains standing armies and other military services. We do not live in a peaceful world. We must recognize then the place of the service man in uniform for his country, whether friend or foe. The man in uniform must be reached with the gospel of Christ. The section deals with Cornelius, but relates the names of and influence of other Christian soldiers, e.g. Dobbie, Washington, Gordon, Montgomery, Eisenhower.

A. *The Seeker and Believer.* 10:1-8; 28-33

In tracing the life of Cornelius there is not much detail given. We know he is a Roman centurion and the background is clear.

(1) Devout (10:1-3). He is seen in a good light in the New Testament picture. Was he a proselyte to Judaism? Is this implied in that he was "God-fearing"? Out of paganism comes this religious man. Many religions were found in Rome and we wonder how he had moved to this special position of seeking the one true religion?

(2) Earnest (10:4-8). His actions in philanthropy and his devotions of worship and prayer were not overlooked by God. These indicated the spirit and motive of the Centurion. He was a disciplined man in his vocation and calling: he is also disciplined in the religious exercises in which he engages. No one need despise the exercises connected with spiritual life. The habit can be the basis of the illumination of the Holy Spirit when he pleases. Cornelius was prepared for the full and final revelation in Christ because his intention was honest and passionate.

(3) Sincere (10:28-33). All that is recorded here shows him to be a man without guile. He is single-minded in all he does. From the beginning of his search to the obedience of faith, Cornelius is portrayed with a character of the best type. Like

the rich young ruler in the Gospels, Jesus must have loved Cornelius when he saw his heart.

B. *The Convert and Missionary.* 10:34-48

The chapter is full of interesting points which reflect how God works in the man to be converted and also in the man who is the channel of bringing Christ.

(1) Social customs divide, but Christ unites (10:28). The idea of a Jew having fellowship with a Roman soldier was something impossible, yet the barriers were removed. It was not necessary for the Roman to become a Jew in order to be a Christian (10:35). The Roman was accepted by God and then welcomed by the Christian (10:34-43).

(2) Christ is the explanation (10:37-38). When Cornelius entered into the full life of the Christian he did so by accepting the Christian message of Jesus. All of Mark's Gospel is here in Peter's address. The outline is clear, the person and work of Christ is given forcefully, and Cornelius accepts and is baptized by the Holy Spirit into the body of Christ. Here was one sermon which was incomplete! Before Peter finished talking, the Holy Spirit fell upon Cornelius and his household (10:44). Because of Holy Spirit baptism (the pouring out — the affusion of the Spirit), water baptism followed. We may not dictate the coming and going of the Spirit in sovereign grace.

This convert was a man under authority. Rome gave him orders. "Jesus Christ: (he is Lord of all)" (10:36). Could it be that when this word was emphasized it met the special need and point of contact for Cornelius? Jesus is the Lord (*ho Kurios*). Rome boasted that Caesar was lord (*kurios*). The Christian faith is that Jesus is the *Kurios,* The Lord. In that hour Cornelius became subject to another King and was forever the servant of another Kingdom, not of this world.

Acts 11

APOSTOLIC MINISTRY

11:1. "the apostles and brethren ... in Judea heard that the Gentiles had also received the word of God."

11:12. "the Spirit bade me go ... nothing doubting."

11:23. "Who, when he came, and had seen the grace of God, was glad."

I. HISTORICAL SETTING. Now that a Roman soldier had become a Christian, the news spread quickly and the Christians of Hebrew background and tradition were concerned. This group, chiefly at Jerusalem, was known as "they that were of the circumcision." They did not like it that Peter kept company with Gentiles. This became an issue eventually to be settled by a council of the church in Chapter 15 but here there was a partial clearing of the tensions when Peter explained what had happened. After his visit to Joppa and Caesarea, he returned to Jerusalem to report to his brethren there. Out of this came the special commission and Barnabas was sent to investigate. Thus the witness of the apostles was vindicated and the church had an understanding of what God was doing by the varied ministry of the Spirit.

II. EXPOSITORY MEANING. Some heard of Peter's revolutionary actions, but they did not understand the meaning of his vision and experience. What had happened to Cornelius was a test case for all.

Acts 11:1. "Also received the word of God." This is the hall mark of genuine Christianity. In that eternal word lies the secret of the power to transform life. Whatever else had come to Cornelius, this was vital — the word of God. No enduring work is done in the soul until that word finds entrance; then the life of God in the soul of man begins to expand.

Acts 11:3. "Thou wentest in to men uncircumcised, and didst eat with them." This was contemptuous expression. Peter was in trouble by the prejudice and judgment of his kinsmen. Taboos and ritualism were involved as religious prejudice dies hard, even today. Many there are who refuse fellowship on various grounds of interpretation of the Christian faith, e.g. Baptism, the Lord's Supper, Orders, Succession.

Acts 11:4. "Peter rehearsed . . . and expounded it by order." The explanation was orderly and reasoned, step by step, so that nothing was omitted. Before Pentecost — how would Peter have replied under the contemptuous pressure? The story of the *facts* is given simply (Acts 11:5-15).

Acts 11:8: "Not so, Lord." He who says "not so" cannot say "Lord." He that says "Lord," will not say, "not so!" Lordship implies obedience.

Acts 11:9. "What God hath cleansed, that call not thou common." There is no distinction between sacred and secular. All life under God is *koinōnia* (the word for fellowship, partnership, communion, oneness).

Acts 11:12. "The Spirit [capital in Greek] bade me go, nothing doubting." This was the compulsion and pressure of God's will in this situation. Six others went, so that Peter was not alone in this. If an angel could stand in the house of Cornelius, surely an apostle might do so?

Acts 11:14. "Words, whereby thou and all thy house shall be saved." The religion of Cornelius did not save him: it was the new message of the Christian gospel.

Acts 11:15. "As I began to speak, the Holy Spirit fell on them . . ." What other evidence was necessary to prove that this was divine?

Acts 11:16. "Then remembered I the word of the Lord." The Spirit was recalling to mind for Peter what Jesus had taught (cf. John 16:13; Mark 1:8).

Acts 11:18. "God also to the Gentiles granted repentance unto life." This is the irrefutable fact.

Acts 11:23. "When he . . . had seen the grace of God, was glad." How grace is seen is obvious in the transformed lives of people. The new spirit among them also endorsed this.

It is good to rejoice when God does something for others
even though it is not the same for us.

Acts 11:26. "They assembled with the church." They
gathered together as a synagogue company with the assembly.

III. DOCTRINAL MEANING. The doctrine of the work of
the Holy Spirit is expressed in the variety of operations in
this section. There is "the regularity of the irregular." Each
group and each convert is touched in a different way. God's
servants are also led in different ways. No one can confine
the Spirit's operations to one method and through one kind
of channel. God breaks through in the new and that which
breaks with tradition.

IV. PRACTICAL AIM. As this marks the watershed of
Christianity or the great divide between Judaism and the
new faith, this chapter deals with the sifting of the minds of
the apostles and brethren in their prejudices and traditions
which hindered. The first Christians were Hebrews, but now
the Gentiles will be in the church of God with them. Should
they be given the same welcome and receive equality of fellowship? Should they be asked to submit to certain Jewish
rites as part of their salvation? Peter's experience with Cornelius paved the way for the final decision which came later.
But the battle was fought here, and from henceforth none
need add anything to the faith reposed in Christ as the Lord
and Saviour of all life. Jew and Gentile when found "in Christ"
ceased to be at enmity or in tension. They were now "one in
Christ" and as such this would be the one norm to decide
who would receive Christian fellowship.

V. HOMILETICAL FORM

Theme: "Apostolic Ministry."

Introduction: The onward progress of the church did not
stop on the borders of the Roman Empire. The commission
of the Lord was carried out to all peoples. Here is another
step forward and onward. After Cornelius and Caesarea come
Phenice, Cyprus, and Antioch. The map should be consulted
for each location and the stretched out line of Christian witness is ever widening. Note here the work of the witnesses in
this particular.

A. *Their Preparation.* (11:1-18)

No work for God is lasting which does not receive adequate preparation. Planning and vision are pre-requisites.

(1) The Report of Peter (11:1-17). Because of the nationalism and parochialism of the early Christians, this was a decisive factor in changing the attitude of the entire church. The news was about Cornelius and the part played by Peter. Peter was thus using "the keys of the kingdom" when he opened the door through the gospel to admit a Gentile soldier into the fellowship.

Peter simply told the story of what happened (11:5-15). The facts spoke for themselves. Because God's orders were clear, what else was there to dispute? Peter did not repeat his sermon when relating the story. He rested his defense on what God did, not on what he said.

(2) The Response of the Church (11:18). This was most heartening. Although at first there seemed to be diffidence and difficulty, nevertheless the church began to understand what had happened and so prejudice gave way to patient, willing understanding. When God has decreed and shown that all men without distinction are welcomed in the church, then fellowship is not narrow and we must accept those whom he has chosen. Thus peace came to the church. At first the Jewish group accepted this as an exceptional case, and it was only later that they saw it as precedent for others.

B. *Their Progress.* (11:19-30)

Leaving Peter and the others in Jerusalem we now move out to other parts of the Roman Empire. The ever widening witness continues.

(1) Early missionaries (19-21). Because of the scattered Christians the gospel had been carried to other parts of the Mediterranean. A new base of operations now came into significance. Check Antioch on the map. It was known for its literature, art, religions, and commerce. It was infamous for vice and frivolity.

The scattered witnesses (cf. 8:4) touch this city, next in importance to Alexandria and Rome. Antioch will now supplant Jerusalem as the center of Christianity. When the heathen (Greeks not Greek-speaking Jews) are won for Christ, the church at Jerusalem sends Barnabas to report on the affair.

(2) Barnabas (11:22-24). This man was always doing the right thing at the right time (cf. 4:36; 9:27; 11:23-24). In each case he is helping someone in need and especially standing by one who is ostracised. Grace brings gladness. A smaller man would have raised difficulties about tradition and ritual. Barnabas was a man of persistence — "cleave" — and he recognized when people set themselves — "purpose of heart" — to go on in the Christian life.

As a character he was blessed with integrity "a good man"; spirituality "full of the Holy Spirit"; and fidelity "full of faith." He was balanced and wise.

(3) Saul (11:25-26). Barnabas sought out Saul and joined forces. Barnabas was not jealous of God's choice of Paul. He did not see him as a rival but as a brother and fellow worker in Christ. He was God's man for the emergency.

This was a famine year and trouble lay ahead. What a rich time the Antioch congregation had before Barnabas and Saul left them! Two great-hearts served the church for a whole year. Think of the Old Testament Scriptures being studied and expounded and the unfolding of Paul's gifts as a teacher. The church grew and many were added to the Lord because they "turned" [epestrephen] (11:21).

At Antioch the followers of Jesus were nicknamed "Christians" and the name abides today. Think of what the New Testament has to say about being a Christian.

Barnabas and Saul are then sent back to Jerusalem with gifts for the needy there in time of famine-relief. Relief was given by disciples in Antioch — "according to his ability" [euporeito] (11:29). The relief was the service rendered in Christ's name and spirit. In all this, whether evangelizing, winning one to the kingdom, teaching the church, or sending relief — this was the witness of the whole church to the whole world.

Acts 12

THE CHURCH UNDER TOTALITARIANISM

12:1-2. "Herod ... killed James ... proceeded further to take Peter."

12:4. "intending after Easter."

12:11. "the Lord ... hath delivered me out of the hand of Herod."

12:23. "the Lord smote him [Herod]."

12:23. "the word of God grew and multiplied."

I. HISTORICAL SETTING. As the church spread out from Jerusalem and began to infiltrate the whole of Palestine and then widen out to the rest of the Roman Empire, the opposition resumed its strength and terror. At Jerusalem, where the first Christians had their center, the apostles were in charge. What more natural that the enemy should attack here and seek to destroy its leadership? Peter had already known attempts on his life and imprisonment was nothing new to him. Now came another season of tribulation as the State through its ruler and power sought to wipe out the struggling church in Jerusalem.

II. EXPOSITORY MEANING. This was the third time for Peter to be imprisoned. He had endured other trials (cf. 4:3; 5:18).

Acts 12:1. "Stretched forth" (*epibalen*). This is a vivid way to describe the subtle and cunning method of despotism.

Acts 12:1. "To vex" (*kakōsai*). The act was linked with evil intent and cruelty.

Acts. 12:3. "It pleased the Jews." How evil spreads when there is a bribe or vested interests or some hoped for gain!

Acts 12:4. "Intending after Easter." Passover time implied

that Herod waited eight days before the attempt on Peter. The realm of intention is important — man's intention over against God's purpose.

Acts 12:5. "Kept in prison ... but prayer was made ... for him." In the crisis the church had this one weapon of spiritual power against the might of the state and its tyranny. "Without ceasing." (ektenōs) means "earnestly" the church prayed to God.

Acts 12:11. "When Peter was come to himself." Strange things had taken place. "Now I know." We have the assurance that he understood that God had delivered him out of prison and that it had been no hurried flight from beyond the iron gate. A vivid picture is given of the details. Early morning escape brought him to the house of Mary.

Acts 12:8. "Bind on thy sandals." God did many things Peter could not do in unlocking the cell door, the prison gate, the sleeping soldiers; but Peter could put on his own shoes. God does not perform the unnecessary things.

Acts 12:12. "The house of Mary, the mother of John ... Mark." What memories of that house arise! Was this the place of the Passover and Supper of the Upper Room of our Lord? Was this the meeting place of the first group of Christians?

Acts 12:16. "When they ... saw him, they were astonished." They had prayed for Peter, but now they hardly believed their prayer was answered.

Acts 12:17. "Go show these things unto James, and to the brethren." The leaders of the church and the other members should be told of the miraculous deliverance. James here is the Lord's brother who will preside at the Council (cf Acts 15). James (12:2), the brother of John, was an apostle and killed by Herod. John was spared to old age. Strange are God's providences when tyrants threaten.

Acts 12:18. "No small stir." Ordinary soldiers lose their lives because a Herod is displeased they could not guard him.

Acts 12:20. "Highly displeased ... desired peace." State trouble is also no small stir and Herod must placate his enemies.

Acts 12:21. "Upon a set day Herod." This was the last of the despot. His vanity and oration proudly claimed his idolatry. God's judgment came to smite him with a loathsome disease.

Acts 12:24. "But the word of God grew and multiplied." The end of the persecution is the beginning of propagation in the gospel.

Acts 12:25. "Barnabas and Saul...took with them... Mark." A new recruit is added to serve as an attendant and helper in missions.

III. DOCTRINAL MEANING. The fact of the miraculous should not be discounted at any time. Apostolic Christianity is full of examples of how God intervened in the unusual manner. Men found it difficult to explain how he operated. The supernatural is discounted by many today, yet we live in a world of the marvelous and the mysterious. New Testament revelation includes this. When Peter is delivered from prison, God works silently to overrule the guards, the gate, the chains, the whole system of man's best plan to keep a prisoner. Yet when Peter is free, he must put on his own sandals and robe, and later at the house of Mary he beckons for silence as he explains and then he goes to another house to stay. Human precautions are taken by Peter even though God had worked a miracle. There is the intertwining of the natural and the super-natural in our world.

IV. PRACTICAL AIM. To show that when the church or Christians are under persecution at any time or in any place, there is the sovereign will of God in operation in his providence. In some cases this will mean deliverance in answer to prayer. In other instances it may mean that an apostle like James is killed and yet again that his brother John will outlive everyone to old age and die quietly. When persecuted the church has but one effective weapon and that is to pray earnestly to God.

V. HOMILETICAL FORM
Theme: "The Church under Totalitarianism."
Introduction: The infant church knew the blast of evil

which came from the dictatorial powers of the state. The issues of the first century were centered in the demand of the state to worship the Emperor as the *kurios* or the Lord. In this the citizens of the Roman Empire might have any religion they chose, but everyone must be subservient to this final worship of the god-emperor as the deity. Christians found that they could not acknowledge the emperor in this way and so they were persecuted and killed because of their refusal. They confessed that Jesus the Christ was THE LORD, the *Kurios*. Against terrible odds the church grew, and it grew through its strength to survive this assault on its faith.

A. *The Second Martyr*. 12:12

Stephen was the first named martyr according to the record, but now we read of James, the apostle and brother of John. "About that time" could mean A.D. 44, the date of the death of the grandson of Herod the great. The "vexing" meant to "do evil" and political persecution implied the scourge and prison for Peter. James was one of the sons of thunder (Mark 10:38) and a violent death was anticipated. He is the first apostle to die and his brother John was probably the last.

B. *The Detention of Peter*. 12:3-6

Peter was familiar with the inside of prisons as this was the third time for him. He was well guarded without and within. Our Lord was sacrificed at Passover time, but Herod planned to wait until after. The motives of the individual are crucial. Sixteen soldiers in all; four shifts of six hours each; two soldiers inside chained with the prisoner; two soldiers on the outside — surely every precaution had been taken. This was the crisis hour for the church. Prayer is offered earnestly as if they stretched and strained themselves in agony before God on Peter's behalf. Prison is answered by prayer: the threat of the enemy is matched by uplifted hands of intercession.

Some might well ask, What is the good of prayer? How can prayer change things in a world dominated by military might; atomic weapons of war; tyrants and despots in a totalitarian enslaved world? We may not be able to explain all — but one thing is certain — God works on behalf of those who trust in him.

C. *The Deliverance of Peter.* 12:7-17

This was the act of God. Girded and guarded by God, Peter left the prison without haste or flurry. All the details are eloquent with the sense of the divine activity amid the human frailties of man.

At the house of Mary there is excitement. Some church gatherings are dull and ordinary — but not so when an apostle is delivered as from death. Then prayer has a new meaning, and some do not believe for joy in the incredible. There is humor in the reaction of the servant girl at the door knowing Peter's voice, with the Christians inside who thought she was mad in telling an incredible tale. What had they prayed for? Was it his deliverance or merely that God would be with him?

D. *The Downfall of Herod.* 12:18-25

Nemesis and judgment fall upon the despot. He who fights against God comes to his end surely and finally. Evil has its way, but not forever. Vanity and pride in a man work out to their loathsome end in destroying the whole man. God is not mocked and He will not allow any to take or usurp his rightful place as the only true God to be worshipped. All else is blasphemy. Psalm 2 reminds us that when wicked men become as anti-Christ, then God laughs in heaven and the day of recompense and vindication is not far off.

Paganism in its worst sense of heathen religion and entrenched evil and superstition finds its end. It does not surrender without struggle. Herod in his presumption is typical of the pagan and evil powers of the tyrant. Dr. Luke describes the judgment of God in that Herod was worm-eaten as a tree that is rotten and falls. It was a stroke, the stroke of a holy God against idolatry.

We still fight against totalitarianism and false religion enthroned with it. Only One can be the Lord and He will have his will and way finally. The Christians in the Colosseum; the faithful at the stake and with the wild beasts; the flaming torches of Nero's gardens; the followers of Christ who endured in concentration camps and the persecutions around the world today find this Scripture relevant. The Hitlers and the Herods, the Neros and the Stalins pass, but the Church prays and prospers, and Christ reigns forever.

Acts 13

NO MISSIONARY SOCIETY

13:2. "Separate me Barnabas and Saul for the work."

13:3. "They sent them away."

*13:4. "So they, being sent forth by the Holy Spirit ...
sailed."*

I. HISTORICAL SETTING. As the story is recorded Christ's
men expand their work from the center to the circumference
of the world of that day. Acts 1:8 was fulfilled in ever increasing measure as the message was taken from province to province and from city to city. Now begins the first missionary
journey, to be followed by others. The church is no longer
anchored at Jerusalem but is thrust out into the whole world.
Gradually through the experience of Peter, and eventually
through Barnabas and Saul, the church has come to the place
of utter abandonment to the commission given to "go to all
the world."

II. EXPOSITORY MEANING. The chapter here is the unfolding of the opening verses and carries the commentary upon the outgoing of the missionaries.

Acts 13:1. "There was in the church ... at Antioch." The
distinction and honor of the missionary thrust was that of the
Antioch church. Jerusalem waited too long or hesitated
through disobedience. The glory of taking the gospel to the
whole world belongs first to Antioch.

Acts 13:1. "Certain prophets and teachers." Where did
they come from? Were they raised up of God in that particular congregation? Saul and Barnabas had come from outside.
The others in name are interesting. Three prophets first.
Was Simon (Niger) related to the Simon who bore the Cross
of Jesus? Was Lucius an evangelist? (cf. Acts 11:20). Two

teachers are listed. Could Manaen come from the Court of Herod? The gospel reaches the highest in the land. Saul is last.

Acts 13:2. "As they ministered [*leitourgountōn*] to the Lord, and fasted." This has the idea of the "liturgical" order of worship. God calls in strange ways and hours. He chooses his servants as He wills.

Acts 13:2. "The Holy Spirit said" — not of man, but of God. "Separate me ... for the work." The two called ones were set apart by God himself.

Acts 13:3. "When they had fasted and prayed, and laid their hands on them they sent them away." A period of self-examination and dedication in prayer to be equipped was vital. The laying on of hands did not confer anything special but was an outward and visible sign of recognition that God had called. The church endorsed what God had revealed.

Acts 13:5. "They preached the word of God." This was the method of evangelism and missionary work. They communicated and proclaimed the Good News.

Acts 13:5. "John departing from them returned to Jerusalem." How short a time he spent with them. Why his deflection? Was it fear or cowardice or physical inability to meet the new demands? No explanation of this seeming desertion is given.

Acts 13:15. "Any word of exhortation" [*paraklēseōs*]. The word that brings comfort and strength because it is a word alongside as a paraclete is.

Acts 13:27. "Every sabbath day." Think of all the services and the worship with its reading of Scripture.

Acts 13:32. "We declare ... glad tidings." Actually, we evangelize you.

Acts 13:43. "Now when the congregation was broken up." What happens after the congregation disperses after service?

Acts 13:48. "As many as were ordained to eternal life believed." Ordained *(tetagmenoi)* — means that they were among the elect, the chosen ones.

Acts 13:51. "They ... came unto Iconium" — the place of the stones.

III. DOCTRINAL MEANING. That only those who are called by the Holy Spirit are able to go forth to spread the Good News and also meet the opposition involved. Also that the church in its regular worship must be sensitive to the spiritual moments when the Spirit is laying hold of individuals for special ministries. The congregation will ultimately ordain and send forth those recognized, but the prerogative of choice is with God and not man.

IV. PRACTICAL AIM: The church must learn that only as a missionary agency does the church survive and justify her existence. The early church did not organize a missionary society as such. Every Christian was thrust into the place of responsibility in evangelism. Every member was expected to be a witness for Christ. Whatever the daily occupation there was the field of service. When special ministries were necessary, as in sending some to distant parts, then the hand of God was laid upon chosen ones for that task. But the church as a whole was the missionary society.

V. HOMILETICAL FORM

Theme: "No Missionary Society."

Introduction: This was a momentous hour in the history of the church. At Antioch the destiny of the rest of the Roman Empire was met by the willing dedication of selected men for special tasks in distant places of the earth. How beautifully the story unfolds as God calls this one and the other to missionary service.

A. *A Missionary Church.* 13:1-2

This is vital and needs to be stressed repeatedly, that we see here the kind of church and congregation planned and willed from the beginning. Here are the principles for the services and task of the whole church.

(1) Leaders of the church (13:1) are listed. These men who were prophets and teachers had a ministry within the church already. They expounded the Old Testament Scriptures and led in worship. They foretold the truth and taught the people who were gathered in from the heathen world around. They were men of dedication and gift and came from all walks of life.

(2) Leading of the Spirit (13:2). God's call cannot be standardized. The voice of the Spirit reaches men in various ways. Some hear it at work; some in meditation; some in prayer. Here, it came during the exercises of public worship and as they were carrying out the liturgical order. To be separated unto God is to be set apart for His will and purpose in life.

B. *Valedictory.* 13:3-4

When the time came for the departure of the two selected men, Barnabas and Saul, the whole church shared in this. Their consecration of life was seen that when God called they obeyed, and no man dared forbid. What a service that would be when the missionaries were ordained and sent forth! This should be part of the experience of all churches so honored to give its best young life to special service.

The map is helpful to see the circuit they were to follow. Thrust out by the divine Spirit, they were bidden to go with the blessing and prayers of the church. They went as representatives of the church and they labored always as belonging to the church and not independent of the church. They would return to the church and report by and by.

C. *Outward Bound.* 13:5-52

Just as these men did not leave Antioch unheralded and unnoticed, so they were to be given publicity wherever they went. Not that they sought this, but the nature of the task brought it on them. Their presence in other communities and cities stirred up others when they presented the claims of Christ.

As they leave Antioch they take John Mark with them as their assistant and attendant. They went to Seleucia on the coast, then to the island of Cyprus, where they encountered the mountebank and false teacher. The public controversy gave Paul an opportunity to show the right ways of God and the wrong ways of men. From Cyprus they went to Perga in Pamphylia, where John Mark leaves them and returns home. No explanation is given for his conduct. Was it the perils of the highlands of Asia Minor, an unwillingness to expose himself to the dangers and rigors of that lot? Perhaps II Corinthians 11:26 throws light upon this as found in Paul's journeys.

Sir William Ramsay thinks that "Mosquitoes gave him (Paul) malaria at Perga." At any rate the two friends went on in spite of the dangers and hazards. Leaving the lowlands for the highlands (cf. Gal. 4:14; II Cor. 12:7), the missionaries reached Antioch in Pisidia.

The map will take us by highway and sea from Antioch to Salamis; to Perga; to Antioch Pisidia; then to Iconium. This is the circuit outward bound and marks a stage in the missionary enterprise.

In the midst of Paul's address is the germ of what he later expanded into the themes of the letters to the Romans and to the Galatians. "By Him justified" (13:39) is that key sentence. This obviously was the heart of their message in every place.

In the synagogue he stressed God's mercy and justifying grace in Christ. The hostility of unbelieving Jews compelled Paul to center his efforts in Antioch on the Gentiles (13:46). Results followed, but Paul was hounded by prejudice until he and Barnabas left under protest (13:51; cf. Matt. 10:14). In contrast, there was joy in the spirit — led disciples who had believed. Outward bound had its risk, but the church was justified in its venture.

Acts 14

THE COST OF MISSIONS

14:5. "There was an assault made ... to stone them."

14:19. "Having stoned Paul ... supposing he had been dead."

14:21. "They returned to Lystra."

14:27. "They rehearsed all that God had done."

I. HISTORICAL SETTING. The church had reached out through its servants and was now spreading the gospel around the eastern part of the Roman Empire. Outward bound as the missionaries were, meant that they touched many places of importance. The map helps to evaluate their journey. Not every place welcomed them, although they were given a hearing at the first. Some success came their way when people responded to their message. At this stage of the enterprise, they had reached a place from which they were to return to the home base. Rural districts were to be touched as well as strategic centers of population. At this juncture they face fierce opposition and yet they elect to return by the same places where the enemies of the faith were against them.

II. EXPOSITORY MEANING. In estimating what it takes to affect a beachhead for missions there are costs involved.

Acts 14:1. "Jews, and Greeks believed." This was encouraging when diverse peoples were united in Christ. The synagogue was the place of contact for Jews, although there were those who opposed and disbelieved.

Acts 14:2. "Stirred up ... made their minds evil affected against." Nothing is more poisonous than prejudice and evil rumor. Think of all the hatreds among people stirred up by false propaganda. When the mind is brainwashed for evil ends, then we have the battle for the mind facing us when we present the Christian Faith.

Acts 14:4. "Multitude ... divided." A divided people is dangerous.

Acts 14:5. "Assault made ... to stone them." No welcome committee here!

Acts 14:15. "We . . . are men of like passions with you." A mistaken supposition was responsible here. Because God had done something extraordinary, people wrongly concluded that the missionaries must be as gods come among them. They were not more than other people.

Acts 14:15-17. "Turn ... unto the living God." He is revealed here as the God of revelation, creation, history, redemption. Revealed religion and natural religion intertwine.

Acts 14:21. "They returned again to Lystra" — back to the place of the stones!

Acts 14:22. "Confirming ... exhorting" — bringing strength and courage for growth in discipleship.

Acts 14:23. "Ordained ... elders in every church." Churches founded as separate congregations are given leadership by presbyters from among the people. Ordination was by the laying on of hands.

Acts 14:26. "Sailed to Antioch, from whence they had been recommended." What emotions as they return! "Recommended" (paradedomenoi) implied they had been commissioned.

Acts 14:27. "Gathered the church together" — a welcome home meeting. "Rehearsed [aneggellon] all that God had done." They told the good news of missionary evangelism and gave report.

III. DOCTRINAL VALUE. One of the doctrines to be taught in the Christian life is that of perseverance. The saints must persevere in their faith and also in their lives. When tested and tried, when opposed and attacked, then the Christian learns the worth of faith under attack. There is a price to be paid, there is a cross to bear for Christ's sake. Suffering and loss are part of the Christian life and not always is there success or ease or protection. We suffer and one day we shall reign with Christ. Missionaries who go to the unknown and untraversed know that there is some cost to their labors. A beachhead on the enemy's territory cannot be achieved without suffering and sacrifice.

IV. PRACTICAL AIM. To encourage Christians to think of the Christian life in terms of reality and not sentiment. There is a romantic flavor about many missionary hymns and many in the church imagine that Christianity is a soft and easy life. We are called to endure hardship as good soldiers of the Cross (II Tim. 5:13).

There is also this important value that Christians should not give in or give up easily when confronted with opposition or discouragment. There is the spirit that can endure and "take it" and the church cannot surrender to the enemy by retreats. We need to go back where we were attacked and face again the old situation and the enemy on his territory. Victories of faith can be won at the point where we seemed to be thwarted and hindered.

V. HOMILETICAL FORM

Theme: "The Cost of Missions."

Introduction: What a thrilling story this is! Imagine the missionary service when the church at Antioch sent out the missionaries when they had commissioned them to go. They left on their circuit overseas. They moved from place to place in hope and expectancy. Many responded to the message, but now there is opposition and assaults upon their lives. Do they give up? No; for here is the story of how they went back by the same way where they were opposed. To face again the old difficulties is not easy, but possible.

A. *The Circuit Overseas.* 14:1-20

Trace from the map the various places and districts wherein they labored. Rural districts and strategic centers of cities were included. Language barriers would arise sometime.

(1) Iconium (14:1-5). The partnership of missions is a rich experience. When discouragement comes Barnabas and Paul need each other. In the disobedient (14:2) we see that those who dislike God's Word are those who disobey it. Barnabas and Paul are called "apostles" (14:4) — the first use of

the word apart from the original Twelve Apostles. The meaning of the word *apostolos,* "sent one," is fulfilled in them as missionaries.

(2) Lystra (14:6-20). The memories of this town would never be erased from the minds of the missionaries. Here they encountered the stones and here they were thought of as gods! The cripple who was healed little thought that this miracle would begin the upheaval it did. The cure was effective and the superstitious people imagined that the gods had come down to assist them. This was an opportunity for the missionaries to present their message. It brought out that God was the God of creation and of history. Natural and revealed theology are here. How easily the pendulum swings when a crowd is swayed. After deification comes opposition and hatred. Danger is here as it has been for missionaries throughout the centuries in every land.

B. *Homeward Bound.* 14:21-25

The thoughts of home bring emotion to those who are abroad in strange places. What must it have been for the missionaries on this first journey into the unknown? Here the places are named as they move homeward, Derbe, Lystra, Iconium, Antioch, Pisidia, Pamphylia, Perga, Attalia. They returned by the same route, instead of a nearer way. Why the longer road and why this strange decision? Lystra was the place of the assault and stones. Paul and Barnabas do not bypass this place. They return to face the stones again if necessary; the threats of Iconium; and the expulsion of Antioch Pisidia. There is a reason.

In this act we see the divine strategy for missions. Missions is a costly business. Many lonely graves of women, children, and men testify in all lands when a beachhead must be made in the enemy's territory. The cost is not in money alone. Lives are expendable. Thus Paul and Barnabas faced again the old difficulties and threats against their lives. But more — they went back because they would strengthen the converts there; confirm the faith of new disciples; give extra encouragment to those who recently came out of heathenism into Christianity. Not only that, but they also went back to appoint elders or congregational leaders in every church. Such ordination was by the laying on of hands and prayer in setting chosen men apart. The elder or presbyter is the same as the overseer or bishop over a congregation. Was this the beginning of church organization? This was the deposit of Paul and Barnabas in the new churches.

C. *The First Missionary Meeting.* 14:26-28

Home again at Antioch there is the welcome and now the thanksgiving to God for all that had been done in His name. What an inspiring meeting with Paul and Barnabas as speakers!

The gathered congregation eagerly awaited the report. "Rehearsed" implies that they reported in detail — they spelled it out simply and clearly — not what they had done, but what God had done. It was a long and thrilling story. "The door of faith" had been opened to the whole world. The gospel had won many converts and new disciples. Churches had been established. Indigenous, yet they were allowed to have men from among them to lead according to the Spirit's guidance and choice.

The cost of missions is seen in the dedication of lives, in the sufferings endured, in the sacrifices made, and in the spirit to face again the assault of the enemy in every place. To breach the territory of Satan is not easy and missionary work is more than human energy: it must have divine power working in and through the missionaries. But "men of like passions" — ordinary men can be tools of God for his enterprise.

Acts 15

TURNING POINT OF HISTORY

15:1. "Except ye be circumcised . . . ye cannot be saved."

15:3. "The conversion of the Gentiles."

15:11. "We believe that through the grace of the Lord Jesus Christ we shall be saved, even as they."

15:28. "It seemed good to the Holy Spirit and to us."

I. HISTORICAL SETTING. This is one of the crucial sections of the book. It brings us face to face with momentous decisions. These decisions affected not only the early church but have influenced the whole church in every age. This was a pivotal occasion, a time when Christianity definitely moved away from being an off-shoot (merely) of Judaism and became a universal faith and life. The council or assembly called to meet at Jerusalem was fraught with destiny. The phenomenal success of the church at Antioch and of its missionary outreach raised the question of the terms on which Gentile converts should be admitted to share the fellowship of Jewish converts. A section of the church, mostly of Jewish background, wished to insist that submission to the Mosaic Law and ritual was a necessity. But the more liberally-minded group opposed this and said that the Hebrew demands were not necessary. The council convened to settle the dispute.

II. EXPOSITORY MEANING. The discussion which ensued gave ample room for differences of opinion. Decisions were finally made under the guidance of the Holy Spirit as minds were enlightened in God's methods of work among people.

Acts 15:1. "Except ye be circumcised . . . ye cannot be saved." This attempt to foist Hebrew usage upon Gentile converts failed. The argument or prejudiced point of view is one that arises from time to time. Religious groups seek to add something to the simplicity of saving faith. Sometimes it is religious ordinances; penances; works; or belonging to a special group. Whatever is substituted is not needed according to faith.

Acts 15:2. "No small dissension and disputation." We should not be surprised at debate in a Christian assembly. This is the place for expressing different points of view. Some are afraid of controversy, but the church has always been in controversy (*staseōs* and *zēteseōs*).

Acts 15:3. "The conversion of the Gentiles." The expression *tēn epistophēn* is only used here in The Acts. Its use is common and the fact implied in The Acts. The book is full of examples of conversion. The varieties of this experience are noted.

Acts 15:5. "There rose up certain of the sect of the Pharisees." The idea of groups, parties, and denominations is not far away even at the first. Theological differences arise. They need not divide brethren, but some do.

Acts 15:6. "To consider of this matter." The word *eidein* means, to look into.

Acts 15:9. "No difference." Peter's testimony is good. God has made no exceptions when it comes to saving men — one way, one people.

Acts 15:10. "Put a yoke." This has taken place for some. Burdens of religion and social demands spoil many for the gospel.

Acts 15:11. "Through . . . grace . . . saved." This is the basis of all New Testament salvation. Later writings of the New Testament expound this thesis.

Acts 15:19. "My sentence is" (*krinō*). My judgment is.

Acts 15:20. "We write unto them." First letters or decrees are sent.

Acts 15:24. "Troubled you with words." How true this has been! Words, words have been the basis of misunderstanding.

Acts 15:25. "Chosen men . . . with our beloved Barnabas and Paul." How these latter have advanced in the esteem of the church!

Acts 15:26. "Men that have hazarded their lives." They risked death itself for the sake of their Lord *(paradedōkosi,* risked-neck).

Acts 15:28. "Seemed good to the Holy Spirit, and to us." When the divine and the human are one in a right judgment.

Acts 15:29. "That ye abstain from." Fasting becomes a Christian. Where is self-denial and self sacrifice? Some things are out for the Christian if he is to witness effectively in society.

Acts 15:30. "They delivered the epistle." Was this one of the early letters of which we have no copy in detail? The substance is given here. This epistle is from the church at Jerusalem to the church at Antioch.

Acts 15:36. "Let us go again" — the true spirit of the missionary!

Acts 15:37-39. "Barnabas determined to take ... John ... Mark ... Paul thought not good to take him with them." Mark had been the occasion of trouble and separation by these two Greathearts. Both were right and both were wrong. The contention *(paroxusmos)* was provoking; it brought separation. Later, Paul will again accept Mark, and Mark will make good and write the Gospel after his name. God will overrule the division and work out some other diffusion of the gospel thereby.

III. DOCTRINAL VALUE. All decisions of a Christian Assembly should be seen in this light. The Jerusalem assembly made history and set forever the standards for Christian faith and practice. The way of salvation is clear and plain. It is not of works and nothing of religious ritual is to be added. Yet there is also given a decree or recommendation that the Christian life should be lived in purity and without any compromise with evil or idolatry. This is the initial thinking about Christian doctrine, and theology is set forth in formulating how Christians should behave as well as believe.

IV. PRACTICAL AIM. Guidance is required in every age. The principles of truth and of revelation abide unchanging, but social and national standards vary from age to age and from country to country. Christians need aid in making decisions about moral behaviour and Christian witness. Not all Christians act in the same way. Customs of culture, society, family, nationality, and background affect how we express our faith. In this there is liberty, even as at the heart of the faith there is unity and unanimity that only the grace of God saves in Christ.

V. HOMILETICAL FORM

Theme: "Turning Point of History."

Introduction: The first Christian Assembly met in Jerusalem. There the church gathered partly in a local sense and yet with others from other churches. When Antioch was disturbed about the basis of salvation, then Paul and Barnabas were sent to Jerusalem to confer with the leaders there, the apostles and elders. No one realized how decisive that would be.

A. *The Occasion.* 15:1-5

Out of controversy can come good results. All division is not necessarily evil. Today's emphasis for uniformity and union has some merit when it means unity of faith and spirit, not simply organization. In unity there can be diversity and harmony in separate groups. We should not be afraid to *discuss* our faith and the implications of the Christian life.

Religious tyranny and slavery are always a peril. Some religious groups today would bind others into one mould and make them conform if they had the power. Legalism arises periodically and political expediency binds many through its religious code. The battle for religious freedom has to be fought again and again.

B. *The Conference.* 15:6-12

Discussion was not limited to the Apostles as leaders. Elders were present. This foreshadowed the democratic ideal of assembly wherein both pastor and elder, religious leader and the laymen are one in representation and voice. No hierarchy is envisaged here at Jerusalem. Even Peter speaks with deference and pleading. For a former Jew to say there is no difference between Gentile and Jew, now in Christ, is remarkable! Throw off the yoke of bondage, but accept the yoke of Christ. No one is saved by circumcision or any religious rite. Then why ask the Gentiles to be circumcised when the missionaries testify that all men are saved the same way?

C. *The Decisions.* 15:13-21

The presiding officer was James, the Lord's brother after the flesh. Once an unbeliever he was now a convinced Christian through the Resurrection of Christ. Is he leader and bishop at Jerusalem Church? His speech reviews history and how God is calling out a new nation and people, the assembly-church. Impressive as he talks, he finally gave the decision of the group.

D. *The First Christian Letter or Epistle.* 15:22-41

Here is history being made. We are familiar with the New Testament epistles or letters. Was this one lost? What did it contain beside the brief digest given here by Luke the historian? What other words were in it of interest? Was it copied for others?

The early Assembly was warned about the trouble through "words". Of course, all assemblies and conferences deal in "words." Somewhere beneath the welter and plethora of words some word and some truth emerges clearly. This was so now. Endorsement was made of the men who risked their lives for Christ. Divine guidance was accepted in decisions made. A decree was issued to express the mind of the whole church gathered in council. The church at large was asked to heed the recommendations.

The assembly ended; the missionaries or commissioners departed: joy sprang up from grateful hearts; only the trouble between two friends stains the page. Yet in all this we learn that no one is without fault and no one in the church has all the answers. It needs fellowship and partnership in all humility. Over it all God will yet work out his redeeming purpose for all men through the church. As in the first century the battle for freedom was fought and won, so in the sixteenth century it was fought by Luther and others. We, too, are vigilant lest we have to fight the same battle again in our day against religious, social, political forms of tyranny which would take away our spirtual freedom.

Acts 16

VARIETIES OF CHRISTIAN EXPERIENCE

16:1. "a certain disciple . . . Timothy."

16:5. "forbidden . . . to preach the word in Asia."

16:10. "we endeavored to go to Macedonia."

16:14. "Lydia . . . whose heart the Lord opened."

16:30. "What must I do to be saved?"

I. HISTORICAL SETTING. As the church continued to make its way through storm and trouble God led the missionaries in unusual ways. Not every door which seemed open was allowed to be entered. God had plans for the whole world of that day and it was necessary to see providential leading at work. As the missionaries, Paul and Silas, returned with the decisions of the Jerusalem council, they reported to the churches from whence they had come. They were then ready to embark upon a new venture in the East and move more into Asia. Then it was that they were diverted by divine pressure of spirit and by providential events to turn West and so to Europe with the gospel.

II. EXPOSITORY MEANING. From Asia Minor to Europe is not far in miles across a narrow stretch of sea, but to those who crossed, it was a big step of faith in the evangelization of the world of that day.

Acts 16:1. "A certain disciple . . . Timothy" — soon to be known as Paul's son in the faith and a faithful companion and fellow-worker. The letters to young Timothy unveil much for the church. They must have come out of this time of ferment when the church was advancing and developing in organization and leadership. Trace Timothy's conversion, his background, and his service life.

Acts 16:3. "Circumcised him." After Acts 15 with its Council one would imagine this not necessary. But Paul would not have any prejudice against Timothy spoil his usefulness.

Acts 16:4. "Delivered them the decrees" (*ta dogmata*). These formulated decisions were decisive and were to be shared among all the churches as counsel for moral standards and religious life among the younger churches. As a letter or epistle, much more than the usual writing? Apostles and elders at Jerusalem still carried some influence among the new churches.

Acts 16:5. "So were the churches established ... increased in number daily." This is the divine order. Faith must be built up; then expansion by missionary effort to establish new groups constantly.

Acts 16:7. "Forbidden of the Holy Spirit ... Asia ... Bythinia." God does not allow his servants to choose for themselves.

Acts 16:9. "A vision ... a man of Macedonia ... Come over ... help us." Was this in sleep as a dream or was it concretely the work of Dr. Luke, the Greek, who was with Paul and who himself could plead for his native country? God has a variety of ways to call us to serve.

Acts 16:13. "Where ... prayer was wont to be made." Why outside the city and by a riverside? Perhaps this was a small group of women alone?

Acts 16:14. "A certain woman ... Lydia" — a convert who is a business woman. "Whose heart the Lord opened." Here we see the quiet work of the Spirit leading the soul into full life and knowledge of God in Christ.

Acts 16:20-21. "These ... trouble our city ... and teach customs." How true that the gospel brings a ferment to stir up people with its truth!

Acts 16:25. "At midnight ... sang praises unto God." To sing in the night of trouble is not easy, but Christianity brings a song.

Acts 16:30-31. "What must I do to be saved? ... Believe." The most important question is here. It is answered in one way, personal relation.

Acts 16:38. "When they heard they were Romans." Because Paul was a Christian did not mean he surrendered his national, citizenship rights.

III. DOCTRINAL VALUE. The doctrine of conversion is one that needs constant study and elucidation. The varieties are apparent. At the heart of this experience is faith in Christ. The work of the Spirit of God is sovereign in operation, but the accidents of how and when this takes place is as mysterious as the wind in its breath and coming and going. The Spirit's ministry of conversion is vital. So also is the Spirit's ministry of guidance when He leads Christians in their service to one place and another. Doors shut and others open. No one can explain why or how, but the fact is patent.

IV. PRACTICAL AIM. To spread the gospel throughout the entire Roman world meant that someone had to go west and not east. The early church must have been in danger of omitting this vital area of need. Perhaps the leaders were too conscious of the area nearest to them and their attachments as former Jews? At any rate, God thrust out the missionaries into a new world by means of the vision of Macedonia. The church today must keep in mind this constant concern for other peoples and lands so that we lead the world by bringing the gospel to all. If one door closes, another may open.

V. HOMILETICAL FORM

Theme: "Varieties of Christian Experience."

Introduction: God's providence is seen in this story as the gospel is brought to the new world of that day. The church had spread throughout the eastern part of the world and was gradually being established. That was both its strength and its weakness. If established to settle down and think only of itself and its own life, then that was a danger. This event points up the truth that the church is never safe when settled. The church must always have concern for the unevangelized and the unreached areas of the world. The second missionary journey is the occasion of these events.

A. *Paul in Asia Minor.* 16:1-8

(1) He is with Silas and Timothy (16:1-5). Timothy has taken Mark's place. He is of mixed parentage. His back-

ground was a godly home and the knowledge of Scripture. These led to his Christian faith and call to serve. Paul goes with his companions to visit many churches and deliver the decisions of the Jerusalem council. Along the way came the change in direction for ministry.

(2) The Spirit's Constraint (16:6-8). Stopped from venturing farther into Asia, they are now faced with the demand of a new world in the west calling them. David Livingstone sought to go to China but went to Africa. Adoniram Judson tried to enter India but settled in Burma. Doors closed in one area lead to an open door elsewhere. Thus God guides his servants then and now to meet the needs.

B. *Paul in Europe.* 16:9-40

This need of the other continent was brought to the heart of Paul and his companions so that a change in direction was given by the Holy Spirit.

(1) Macedonian vision (16:9-12). Who was the "man of Macedonia"? Sir William Ramsey thinks it was Luke whose home was in Philippi and who joined the group of missionaries. "Concluding" (16:10) suggests that reason and revelation were joined in the decision. One hundred and fifty miles by a straight course at sea implied easy access, yet faith must venture into the unknown and untried area of a Roman outpost.

(2) Conversion of the business woman (16:13-18). The place by the riverside is unusual. Lydia, a business woman from Asia, working with purple dyes and prospering with her work and servants or work-people around her. Her heart is opened and she is converted. What a quiet conversion is this! Paul on the Damascus Road had a cataclysmic experience with blinding light and voice: the Philippian gaoler later will feel the earthquake's shock and cry out in alarm and fear, but Lydia comes quietly, silently, as the sun quietly bathes the flowers with warmth and light. No noise or upheaval, thus are some converted in home and church and Sunday School class.

Lydia is the first convert in Europe and she was from Asia (whence Paul had been forbidden to go)! This conversion led to testimony among her work-people and her home was opened in hospitality. Her home became the place of the new church and the center for Paul in that area. Women like Lydia have done much for Christ and the church.

(3) Conversion of a gaoler (16:19-40). How marked a contrast is this man's change of heart after Lydia. He is brutalized and calloused by his life and work. His outlook is limited and his background is no help. The earthquake is used to shake his inner life into fear and concern. Fear is a powerful motive and should not be discounted in some lives. The sense of impending doom can also move the heart. Paul and Silas are in prison because of their opposition to vested interest and evil. Now is God's way to reach the man in prison. The songs of these two in their indomitable spirit unquenched; the upheaval of the earth tremors; these turned the man into an inquirer. "What must I do to be saved?" has been echoed by many since. It implied "repentance toward God, and faith toward our Lord Jesus Christ" (Acts 20:21).

The new life given to this converted man is seen as he washed the wounds of the missionaries; feeds them; submits to baptism; shares all with his family in joy; and is left to face the authorities with an explanation why he has freed the prissoners! God moves in mysterious ways to bring men to conversion and new life. Little did this man think his story would be told and preached about across the years in testimony! Conversion is right round about from the old life to the new.

Acts 17

CHRISTIANITY AND CULTURE

17:15. "they brought him [Paul] unto Athens."

17:16. "his spirit was stirred in him, when he saw ... idolatry."

17:22. "Then Paul stood in the midst of Mars' Hill."

17:31. "He [God] has appointed a day ... he will judge the world."

17:34. "certain ... believed."

I. HISTORICAL SETTING. Paul and his companions in Europe find their work spreads from Philippi to other cities. They visited Thessalonica and Berea. Finally they come to Athens where we find him encountering the best minds of the Grecian world. Rome might have its military might and its laws; the Jews had their religion and ritual; but the Greeks had a culture, philosophy, and a rich language. Paul soon found himself engaged in tackling the world of culture for Christ.

II. EXPOSITORY MEANING. The setting of this profound scene and story is unforgettable. Geographically it is set amid the monuments of ancient Greece at its best. Architecture and skill had combined to give to the Greeks the best of that day. Allied was philosophy and an inquiring mind, ever questing after truth.

Acts 17:1-2. "Thessalonica ... Paul ... synagogue .... reasoned out of Scriptures." This was dialogue *(dielegeta)* and discussion to point out truth.

Acts 17:3. "Opening and alleging" *(dianoigōn* and *paratithemenos)* — leading into the mind of the hearer, and placing truth alongside to convince.

Acts 17:6. "These that have turned the world upside down."
How true the charge! Christianity must challenge all evil
and be a ferment.

Acts 17:7. "Contrary to the decrees of Caesar." These dogmas *(dogmatōn)* should be compared with the dogmas of the
church (Acts 15:23, 30; 16:4). Christian theology runs counter
to heathen theology.

Acts 17:7. "There is another king, one Jesus." He is the
king of kings (the *basilea*). This was the issue with the state.

Acts 17:11. "More noble" — not higher born, but better-
minded. "Readiness of mind" *(prothumias)* — open minded
and in spirit. "Searched the Scriptures" — thought with dis-
crimination and made a judgment upon Scripture.

Acts 17:15. "Brought Paul to Athens" — not as a tourist
or sightseer.

Acts 17:16. "His spirit was stirred in him." This *(paróxun-
eto)* was a paroxism of feeling, so intense that his whole being
inwardly was tense with emotion and pain. He was so irri-
tated at what he saw that he was angry against idolatry. He
saw the "dead" city.

Acts 17:17. "Disputed" *(dielegeto)* — a debate or dialogue
of question and counter-question aimed to convince.

Acts 17:18. "Certain philosophers." Two kinds are here:
Epicureans with their idea of life with ease, and Stoics with
the ideal of discipline and sometimes sacrifice.

Acts 17:18. "Encountered him" *(suneballon)*. There is a
head on collision here. "This babbler" *(spermoloyos)*. Paul
is called a seed picker, like a bird picking up a scrap here
and there. Not so, Paul!

Acts 17:18. "Preached unto them" *(euaggelizo)*. He brought
them the good tidings.

Acts 17:19. "New doctrine." The teaching *(didachē)* was
new and revolutionary as they found out. New life came
from new teaching.

Acts 17:22. "Too superstitious" *(deisidaimonesterous)* —
very religious (cf. altars).

Acts 17:26. "Made of one blood all nations." This speaks
of the solidarity of the human race.

Acts 17:30-31. "Repent ... judge ... resurrection" — basic notes of gospel.

Acts 17:32. "Some mocked ... hear thee again." This sounds very modern — reject and delay.

Acts 17:34. "Certain ... believed." Fruit abides at Athens, and a church is born.

III. DOCTRINAL VALUE. "What has Athens to do with Jerusalem?" asked Tertullian later, but this is always relevant. What is the connection between the city of philosophy and the city of religion? How can Christianity out of Jerusalem bring truth to culture and education? It does. The doctrine of the Christ who is Alpha and Omega is demonstrated at Athens in the gospel proclaimed. He is Lord of the mind as well as of the heart and life. The intellect must bow to Christ as the Lord.

IV. PRACTICAL AIM. To challenge the philosophers in their seat of learning; to go to college, university, and seminary, and show the superiority of the Christian Faith as the queen of all the sciences. All questions of life are finally theological or spiritual questions and Christ has the answer. To meet also those who are in the market-place and the open forum of debate with the redeeming message for the whole of life; to save the city from idolatry.

V. HOMILETICAL FORM

Theme: "Christianity and Culture."

Introduction: No part of man's life is outside of the gospel of Jesus Christ. This chapter relates to the whole of life as it touches the Christian faith. Whether at Thessalonica or Berea it is the same, but especially at Athens we trace the divine power at work in a human situation.

A. *The Gospel at Thessalonica.* 17:1-9

On the highway of Greece this commercial center was the place of a disorderly mob and Paul was caught in trouble because of his message. A mixed reception awaited him here. Some rejected his message and berated him, even at the same time paying the tribute that "these men ... have turned the world upside down" (17:6). God's work is not in vain. New

life breaks out intermittently in all places. Some of the leading people of that city embraced the new faith and united
with the church.

B. *The Scriptures at Berea.* 17:10-13

Sixty miles further from Thessalonica lay this place associated with those who "searched the Scriptures." Here was a
happy situation where people had an open mind and were
ready to listen and receive the truth. The open mind is an
ally to conviction by the truth. It is a good step toward conversion. The habit of examining the sacred writings is also
another means of conviction. This is the good soil of the
human heart, responsive and ready to take the divine seed.

The right of private interpretation in Bible reading is
linked with this practice of "searching." Let any Christian
read and meditate and knowledge will increase. Not that
every individual will have the final word on the Scriptures:
we must check and share with other Christians so that we will
find general agreement in the truth revealed and recorded.
We dare not dispense with the total witness of the whole
church about the Bible and its study and interpretation.

C. *Comparative Religions at Athens.* 17:14-34

Paul is now at the center of intellectual life, of art, politics,
architecture, and philosophy. Will his message be adequate
here as in other places? Culture is not outside the orbit of
the Christian faith. It can become the handmaid of reason
as mind to faith unite. In Christ are hid all the treasures of
the Godhead; this is the thesaurus from which we draw the
doctrines and truths which will continue to challenge the best
minds of the ages. Divine philosophy and the Christian view
of God and the world are important.

Some think Paul failed at Athens because few are named
as converts. Some incline to judge that his message lacked
the dynamic of the gospel facts, but examination of that message shows he did use the basic truths of redemption. He faced
the indifferent in the agora, the market-place; the pleasure
seeker and the aesthete in the city social life; the pagan cul-
tured man and the ignorant and superstitious with their
altars and idols in the place of the monuments; and he stood

his ground when confronted with those who mocked. Paul had no "scrap of learning" but the philosophy of life which transcended all others and made them secondary to Christ. Colossians 1:12-20 expounds more of that philosophy. Here at Athens he spoke in the outline and summary in the record (17:22-31) as one who was convinced that Christ was the answer to man's quest for truth and beauty.

Paul was kind and courteous in his address and did not omit to notice that the Athenians were "religious" and yet they did not know the "unknown God." He told them about God — Revealer, Creator, Father, Spirit, and the unity of the race; of man's sinfulness and imminent judgment. Paul was acquainted with Greek literature and used it, but his final word was Christ, coming as judge. Acts 17:31 does not omit the gospel facts: it includes them. The resurrection is divine endorsement of the Christ who died to redeem and now lives to reign and judge the hearts of men.

The result was striking (17:32-34). Look at the names of those who responded before we note that some mocked.

A judge in the city court; a woman of importance and rank in the city; and there were "others." This is evidently just a sampling. This became the nucleus of the church at Athens. The witness to the Resurrection of Christ is the power of God to convince men of sin, righteousness, and judgment by the Holy Spirit. The cynic (17:32a); the procrastinator (17:32b) go their way, but the believers (17:33-34) are found to linger. Paul will write to the Greeks at Corinth later (cf. I Cor. 2:1-5) about the difficulty of reaching those who would see nothing but vanity and foolishness in the message he proclaimed, but at Athens some believed. Thus the gospel marches on its way through the world, winning its victories in every situation. Culture bows to Christ and becomes Christian culture, a new mould for a new world order and new creations. Philosophy, art, literature, sculpture, and architecture will yet bring their tribute to the feet of Christ until the world will know that all that is best and true and noble in these spheres has been inspired by Christ.

Acts 18

CHRISTIAN FRIENDSHIPS

18:3. "because he was of the same craft, he abode with them."

18:7. "whose house joined hard to the synagogue."

18:27. "brethren wrote, exhorting the disciples to receive him."

I. HISTORICAL SETTING. Wherever Paul went he made friends. It is heartening to think that friendship is a rich experience within the Christian church. As Paul moved away from Athens he went on to Corinth. Corinth was the chief commercial center of Greece, a cosmopolitan city, a seaport with all its vices and idolatry common in that day. His Jewish kinsmen did not welcome him, so he turns to others who do. During this period there was much opposition. There were contacts with Sosthenes and Gallio, who must have been impressed with the power of Christian witness under duress. Paul became low in spirit and discouraged at one point, but the Lord stood by him. The strain was severe, but the apostle was cheered by the presence of the living Lord.

II. EXPOSITORY MEANING. The conversion in the city of Corinth led to ties of friendship. Paul was glad for the friends he had; and for all that they did for him.

Acts 18:2. "Paul found . . . Aquila . . . with Priscilla." These were Jews who had left Italy. Tentmakers, they shared that in common with Paul.

Acts 18:4. "Reasoned . . . and persuaded" *(dielegeto* and *epeithen)* — the argument of dialogue allied with reasoned speech to influence.

Acts 18:5. "Pressed in the spirit" or "constrained by the word."

Acts 18:6. "I will go unto the Gentiles." Thus Paul broke with his kinsmen. He will give himself wholly to others with the gospel.

Acts 18:7. "Justus ... whose house joined hard to the synagogue" — a pleasing relationship, house and place of worship together.

Acts 18:10-11. "I am with thee." Paul, afraid, discouraged, is now given assurance of God's presence with him. "He continued."

Acts 18:15. "If it be a question of words and names." It must be clear what the charge is, whether civil or religious.

Acts 18:17. "Gallio cared for none of these things." This has nothing to do with his attitude to the Christian message, but rather with his reactions to those who tried to bribe him to act in a matter which he refused to accept as his responsibility.

Acts 18:18. "Paul ... shorn his head ... a vow." How strange all this is after verse 6 in which he cast off his kinsmen!

Acts 18:21. "I must ... keep this feast ... Jerusalem ... but I will return again ... if God will." Which feast? Why did he observe this? The will of God is supreme in life.

Acts 18:24. "Eloquent ... mighty in the Scriptures." Apollos was a man of words and a man of power.

Acts 18:25. "Fervent in the spirit ... taught diligently." His spirit was full of zeal and passion, and he taught with accuracy.

Acts 18:26. "They ... expounded unto him ... more perfectly." They opened up the place of Scripture with accuracy (cf. 18:25 — same word).

Acts 18:28. "Mightily convinced." This was thorough and down in the word; there was power to convince thoroughly.

III. DOCTRINAL VALUE. Christian friendship is a rich experience. The romance of Christian living is found here. As new groups sprang up within the world devoted to Christ, these became the means of breaking down the barriers which separated individuals and nations. Across the prejudice and divisions of race, culture, speech, and religion, there came the one cement to bind people together in unity. Jesus offered salvation which brought his friendship and He called his disciples "Friends." In this new spirit people found each other within the church.

IV. PRACTICAL AIM. This will demonstrate how much we value friendship. Are we sociable or unapproachable? What do we do cultivate friendship within the church? There is friendship evangelism which is most effective. The stranger and the lonely respond to the spirit which diffuses love and warmth of welcome. List some of Paul's friends in the church. It is an imposing list, and includes Barnabas and Mark. There are Silas, Timothy, Luke, Aquila, Priscilla, Titus, Tychicus, Trophimus, Sopater, Aristarchus, Secondus, Gaius, Epaphras, Epaphroditus, Artemas, Apollos, Zenos, Onesiphorus, Pudens, Linus, Claudia, Philemon, Onesimus, and Christians (unnamed) in Rome.

V. HOMILETICAL FORM

Theme: "Christian Friendships."

Introduction: Christians are people who have come out of various backgrounds and now find themselves "one in Christ Jesus." It is inevitable that they find a new alignment with their lives. Whatever friends are ours in the community or through social contacts and work, there is a special area of friendship within the church. There we meet those of like faith and there we work together with those whose aim is the same. Jesus called his first followers "ye are my friends" and ever since the distinction of a friend has been an honor to the Christian. Paul found many friends in his travels.

A. *With Aquila and Priscilla.* 18:1-6

Husband and wife were Jews who had been living in Italy but who had left there under the edict of the Emperor Claudius. As Jews, Paul found a ready contact with them when he came to Corinth. Perhaps no door had opened there among the Jewish people anyway and this was the more welcome. There was also the added reason of their common craft as tentmakers. The Jewish custom in education was sound. "He that teacheth not his son a trade, doth the same as if he taught him to be a thief." Paul then maintained himself by honorable work until Silas and Timothy came from Macedonia with a gift (18:5).

During this period Paul tried to witness to his kinsmen after the flesh. The Jewish community at Corinth was not ready to receive his testimony and resented his message. Think of that vivid and dramatic gesture when he shook his robe and said: "Your blood . . . upon your own heads; I . . . clean." This was not a curse but a sign that he took no more responsibility as he had testified to them.

His friendship with the tentmakers was rich and they must have profited from his presence in the home. Later, they were to assist Apollos. How much was Paul in that?

B. *With Justus and Crispus.* 18:7-11

Justus, a Roman, lived near the synagogue and it is suggested that he had become a believer. Living close to a place of worship can be an asset. Some people live a long way spiritually. It is not a matter of the distance in miles. To have one's daily life joined to God's House is rewarding and when a family is thus related there are dividends to enrich all. Sad for those families who never darken the door of God's House.

Crispus, the leader of the synagogue, also believed in the Christian message as well as other Corinthians. This was encouragement to Paul when he found responses like these. But a storm of opposition was brewing (18:9). Paul was afraid and discouraged sometimes, yet God encouraged him and the promise of Matt. 28:20 was fulfilled in the next eighteen months at Corinth.

C. *With Gallio.* 18:12-17

This well-known man of Rome was mentioned by Seneca. He was the Roman pro-consul. The Jews who were against Paul tried to intimidate him and rush the court. Trouble came by argument. Here is Roman justice, impartial and fair (18:14). Words and hair splitting did not coerce Gallio (18:15). His decision to dismiss the affair opened the door for Paul to preach throughout the whole of the Roman Empire. Sosthenes was blamed (18:17) but later becomes a Christian (cf. I Cor. 1:1). That Gallio "cared for none of these things" does not refer to Christianity, but to the other matters.

Paul found a friend in Gallio and Sosthenes. That day the door was opened wide for him to pass unhindered throughout the world to proclaim his message. What thoughts would Gallio have later in reflection upon the events of that day?

D. *With Apollos.* 18:18-28

The providence that brought this man into the friendship of Paul and his friends Aquila and Priscilla is important. Paul had been to Ephesus and it was there Apollos had come to minister. It was found that he was lacking in part of the full Christian message and needed help. Who would help him? Here is the strange area of friendship which opens the door to two humble people who are tentmakers.

From Alexandria in Egypt came Apollos. That was the center of a university and library. He had a liberal education. He was a scholar and an eloquent preacher of the Scriptures. This is not the usual combination in the scholar. The scholar is often not dynamic and not an enthusiast, although there are the saving exceptions. Scholarship and fervent faith can be wedded together.

Apollos taught accurately what he knew, but he did not know sufficient. His was the message of a limited gospel; it lacked the Cross, the Resurrection, and Pentecost. How modern it sounds! He was competent after the standards of the church, but he lacked the dynamic of the full Christian revelation. He had some facts of truth, but not the fulness of the truth in Christ. Not all truth is the gospel, although the gospel is truth. His teaching had mental adroitness, but, while not erroneous, it missed the essentials to bring men to faith and repentance in Christ. He was clever but not clear. Some today declaim about the life and teaching of Jesus, but these are not enough. We need the Christ who died, rose again, enthroned as Lord of all life and giving us the Spirit to empower life.

Fortunately, Apollos was humble, to sit at the feet of the tentmakers. Strange theological seminary! They expounded the truth to him with accuracy. Here is the picture of friendship within the church. Out of it comes Apollos the orator and expositor of the Scriptures.

Christian friendship brings teacher, elder, deacon, craftsmen, scholar, and preacher to sit together, and work and worship. They are then enriched in the friendship of Christ.

Acts 19

EVANGELISM AND SOCIAL ACTION

19:9. "he ... disputing daily in the school of one Tyrannus."

19:25. "by this craft we have our wealth."

19:27. "not only this our craft is in danger ... but also ... the temple.

19:40. "to be called in question for this day's uproar."

I. HISTORICAL SETTING. When Paul visited the city of Ephesus, he found that evangelism carried several contacts and implications. He visited the synagogue; he used a school room; and he challenged the vested interests of heathen worship. Ephesus was a strategic city serving a large area. When Paul wrote his letter to the Ephesian Church he told of fighting with unseen powers of darkness. He knew from this visit what that meant. This was the setting of an evangelistic thrust when he came.

II. EXPOSITORY MEANING. Evangelism implies the telling of the Good News to everyone. Ephesus proved to be a place of mixed reception and not an easy sphere.

Acts 19:2. "Have ye received the Holy Spirit since [when] ye believed?" To be ignorant of the presence and power of the Holy Spirit was a limiting factor. Paul had left Apollos at Corinth where Apollos had been limited in his experience: now he finds others.

Acts 19:8. "Disputing and persuading" — the dialogue and emotion of winning men for the kingdom of God.

Acts 19:9. "Daily in the school of Tyrannus." This indicated that Paul used the place during the hottest time of the day, when others rested. Probably from 11 a.m. to 4 p.m.

Acts 19:12. "Aprons" (*simikinthia*), the sweat cloths used by the tentmaker. Those who took them had a fitful and darkened faith of a kind (cf. Peter's shadow, Acts 5:15; and the woman who touched the hem of Christ's garment, Matt. 9:20). The Lord meets people where they are, and according to the degree of faith.

Acts 19:19. "Many . . . which used curious arts brought . . . books . . . and burned them." A clean sweep was made of the basis of evil. Unclean was replaced by the pure.

Acts 19:21. "I must also see Rome." This was an apostolic ambition—fulfilled in a strange way later.

Acts 19:9. "Were hardened and believed not"—hardened like gristle and were not persuaded.

Acts 19:23. "No small stir about that way." The stirring up was made by the people of and teaching of the WAY. Way is in capital in the Greek. "Stir" is the word *taraxos*.

Acts 19:25. "By this craft we have our wealth." This is a case of vested interests. Greed of gain and self-interest is involved.

Acts 19:27. "But also . . . the temple." Religious interests were allied to business. One was dependent upon the other.

Acts 19:31. "Certain of the chief of Asia . . . his friends." Again the record speaks of Paul's friends. Trace the names of them in the New Testament.

Acts 19:38. "The law is open." There is a legal way to settle disputes.

III. DOCTRINAL VALUE. Christianity is fully justified when it meets the vested interests of heathenism or any religious practice which is bad. Evangelism takes note of all situations which affect human society. The social application of the gospel is not only valid; it is inevitable wherever Christ comes with new life. The church stands up against the social order which would crucify afresh the Christ and his message. This is the struggle in every generation. We never come to the place where evil is overcome or where there are no more problems to be solved. Christianity goes on facing the tremendous odds as a minority group in the world.

IV. PRACTICAL AIM. This is to encourage and strengthen those in the church who find themselves alone in their struggle. In the Roman Empire the early Christians were a small group and they were called a sect. Lacking much of this world's prestige or wealth, nevertheless the church forced its way into positions of head-on collisions with authority and vested interest, and so demonstrated that Christ was Lord of all life. Nothing could stand up against the church in its ministry. The emperor could not muzzle the missionaries and no prison could daunt their spirit. There was commotion wherever they went.

V. HOMILETICAL FORM

Theme: "Evangelism and Social Action."

Introduction: In our day the church at large has its committees of social education and action. These are also reproduced within the local church in one way or another. By our protests from pulpit, press, and resolution we show that we are concerned about the social conditions under which men live. However, when the Christian man stands up for the Christian message and conviction there are those who oppose. Let a Christian use his political affiliation, or his social friendships, or his business relationship to advance the cause of Christ and there are those who resent this. Yet, the Christian has no option but to apply the teaching of Jesus to every situation involving a moral issue. The church in every age has led in changing social conditions by changing people and then supporting and leading in legislation to improve conditions. The slave trade broken; bringing children and women out of mines; keeping watch on moral needs; this has been part of the church's work.

A. *Working with Jews.* 19:8-9

This is part of evangelism. Jewish evangelism is not always a part of the church today, yet it should be included. By "arguing and persuading" Paul spoke fearlessly and without any reservation. Some "stubborn and disobedient" became like "gristle hardened" and evidently not reached. Christianity is the new WAY, yet some insulate themselves from knowing it.

B. *Preaching to the Public.* 19:10-12

When one group is unresponsive, Paul tries another. When the synagogue is no longer an outlet for truth, then there is a school room to be hired daily. Paul worked as a tentmaker during the early hours of the day. Then, when the heat came and others could rest, he proceeded to lecture in the school-room. How many came? Who responded? Evidently there were some. Two years of this was a good test of the evangelistic spirit. How easily church folk are discouraged, but not so Paul in this case. Evangelism is not for the special hours or the planned campaign. Evangelism must be carried on at all times and in all hours of life to be effective.

Paul met special conditions in that area of need. Some imagined they could be healed and helped through contact with his sweat cloths. God does not endorse superstition, but God will meet the soul at the point of need. Christianity is not in favor of mascots, charms, or any items of superstition, even though religious. Paul saw the books and trinkets of black magic burned and won a victory over evil, over amulets and charms. Where the true faith is found there is no need for fanaticism or fatalism.

C. *Attack upon Vested Interests.* 19:21-34

As Paul wiped out the superstitious charms (19:13-20) ; so now he attacked the more entrenched evil connected with the chief religion of Ephesus. He threw down the gauntlet against rival cults of evil. Spiritual warfare was waged by spiritual weapons, not with carnal weapons. We cannot today win our battles by questionable methods for money or condoning secularized ideas of truth. The magical books were not given away: they were burned! Now against the goddess of Ephesus' temple, Paul engages in one of the fiercest battles of all.

In the traffic for the souls of men there are those like the silversmiths of Ephesus who still shriek about their craft and their wealth. Liquor, gambling, vice, and much else cannot abide the church when the church stands up against entrenched evils. Moral cancers are not dealt with easily. Demetrius appealed skillfully to the people through their pockets and their piety. One of the Seven Wonders of the world stood in Ephesus, but Christ proved to be greater. When religion degrades human life it is wrong and must be excised. Christ is against certain religions. He cuts the nerve of certain businesses.

That Paul was justified in his stand is indicated in the rest of the record. His enemies would condemn and get rid of him, but the State on this occasion protects him. As a Roman citizen he has "rights" and because the church is not allied to the State it is not compromised in any way. Victory comes not by attacking the civic authorities, but by changing lives so that the people then have no more need of or use for idols. "The expulsive power of a new affection" is found here. No longer will the new Christians desire to patronize the heathen temple or buy the mascots made by the craftsmen. Thus vested interests receive a blow which ends in defeat.

Throughout this episode, Paul knew that he "wrestled not against flesh and blood, but against the powers of spiritual wickedness in high places" . . . (Eph. 6:12). The church then and always evangelized when it opposes vested interests, and the church must be involved within the social order to transform it by the gospel.

Acts 20

SERVING THE LORD

20:7. "on the first day of the week, when the disciples came together."

20:18-19. "I have been with you . . . serving the Lord."

20:27. "I have not shunned to declare unto you all the counsel of God."

I. HISTORICAL SETTING. The restless spirit of Paul is noted in his constant travels. These brought him back again to Greece and after a while he returned to Asia Minor. No doubt the needs of the churches impelled him thus to be on the move. He had many to see and much to do. He knew that his days were passing and he must invest all to the full. In Greece he is pleased to find acceptance among the churches and to them he brought exhortation. He spent, in all, three months in Greece on this visit, then came back to Asia Minor in company with several friends (20:5). At Troas, where they landed, memories of an earlier day must have filled his vision. It was there he had received the Macedonian call. He could not see what had happened in the interval but all was worth-while for the gospel's sake.

II. EXPOSITORY MEANING. Human events are part of the divine providence. Some enemies threatening Paul bring about a change of plans.

Acts 20:3. "About to sail into Syria, he." The route was suddenly altered because of the danger. Seven friends are with him on the voyage, and money and administration for the churches are handled by a group and not one individual. They are five days sailing with a delay at Troas.

Acts 20:7. "On the first day of the week"—now the day of the Lord, celebrating the Resurrection. Change from the Sabbath held by the Jews was gradual (cf. I Cor. 16:2). The church meets on this new day.

Acts 20:7. "Breaking bread ... and preached"—two items of church life. The former is not the Lord's Supper (cf. 20:11), and the latter is speaking in dialogue (*dielegeto*), not proclaiming to a crowd.

Acts 20:13, 14, 15. "We went before to ship ... he met with us ... we took him in ... we sailed thence." Luke is Paul's companion, and as the author of this book he relates the story in this fashion.

Acts 20:16. "To be at Jerusalem, the day of Pentecost." How moving an experience to be there then! What insight into the promise and performance of the Spirit!

Acts 20:17. "Called the elders of the church." These had been ordained to leadership and oversight of the assembly.

Acts 20:19. "Serving the Lord with all humility of mind." Humility is second only to love: it is love stooping. "Serving" is the word *douleuōn* — enslaved by the Lord. "Tears and temptations"—the ministry costs!

Acts 20:20. "Kept back nothing ... profitable" (cf. 20:27), "declare ... all the counsel of God." Paul was not a pleaser of men, but he gave them what God revealed.

Acts 20:20. "Taught ... from house to house." The ministry was pastoral in that he went from group to group meeting in homes.

Acts 20:24. "That I might finish my course with joy, and the ministry which I have received." Journey's end comes and the way has its rough spots, but looking back there can be nothing but gladness for the course.

Acts 20:28. "Take heed ... overseers." These elders were the bishops. "Elder" (*presbuteroi,* 20:17), is used as "overseer" (*episkopous*). This was the office of those who led the local church.

Acts 20:28, 29. "Feed the church ... the flock." They were to act as under-shepherds, giving pasturage to the sheep.

Acts 20:28. "The church of God which he hath purchased with his own blood." The daring figure, arresting, concerning the "blood"—the reality of God in Christ. God was in Christ at the Cross. "Purchased" (*peripoiēsato,* not the word to "redeem") , but the word for the shepherd laying down his life for the flock.

Acts 20:31, 32. "Watch . . . warn . . . word." It is important to follow the injunction from one whose tears were spilled for them.

Acts 20:33. "I have not coveted." There is no greed or avarice here. Not lusted after with passion.

Acts 20:34. "These hands"—toiling hands.

Acts 20:34. "Ministered" (*hupēretēsan*) as under-rowers in a ship and as an assistant.

Acts 20:35. "Remember the words of the Lord Jesus." These are extra Scriptural words not recorded in the Gospels. They were passed on and down by oral transmission from those who heard the Lord. To give is the heart of the gospel.

Acts 20:38. "sorrowing . . . see his face no more." The end comes, the last good-bye is spoken!

III. DOCTRINAL VALUE. This section treats of the Christian ministry. In it are the truths bearing upon the pastor or elder or bishop who oversees a Christian congregation. There are high and holy ideals set forth here and in practice they are demonstrated in Paul's experience. His farewell address to the elders at Miletus is full of suggestion.

IV. PRACTICAL AIM. As no church thrives without its members, no congregation progresses without good leadership from those we call the laymen. There is place for pastor or teacher, but the elder is one set apart to lead and guide the church. Some elders become teaching elders and others remain as ruling elders. The men and women who serve the churches are devoted and dedicated people who advance the kingdom of God in and through their service.

V. HOMILETICAL FORM

Theme: "Serving the Lord."

Introduction: Christian service is varied and widespread among churches. The church at the beginning was not conceived of as any building or group of buildings. It was composed of groups of people and this group was the image in

the minds of the community around. For the most part they
met in homes and so were small groups in fellowship. However, as these groups were planted and organized they increased in number, and gradually came church organization
and leadership. Paul appointed leaders everywhere so that after
his departure the work would continue as the Holy Spirit led.
The spirit in which Paul served is unfolded in this chapter.

A. *A Week at Church.* 20:6-12

At Troas, where he had received the Macedonian call, Paul
now spent one week with the Christians. What a rich fellowship is suggested. For a week he preached to them and each
day brought its joy in service.

Special days are noted. "Days of unleavened bread" (20:6)
is Passover, and "Pentecost" (20:16) is mentioned. The church
had its calendar of the Church Year developing, but every
day was a saints' day in the fellowship. Each day the church
progressed in adding others. Each day was a day of evangelism.
The church might lack prayer books, but they prayed. Without the Scriptures (except some Old Testament and a few
letters being written) they confessed their faith and proclaimed their message. They knew how to sing and cultivated
the graces of the Spirit.

The Christian assembly or church gathering came on the
first day of the week. This came gradually and was by use and
conviction, not legislation. Devotions came at night, and Paul
would not start his journey on the Sabbath lest he offend the
Jews; therefore at sunset after the beginning of their day he
would leave, after saying good-bye. The upper chamber indicates a home of some means; the lamps were remembered as
a detail; the long discourse, reading the Scriptures, the supper.
Paul conversed as in a homily (we wonder what was his subject and text?) . That a young man fell asleep is not surprising
—the heat, crowd, smell of lamps, late hour, long talk—perhaps Eutychus tired after outdoor work? Sermon interrupted
—continued again: second part from midnight to dawn. Paul's
informal way of talk noted. What a week!

B. *Farewell to Ephesian Elders.* 20:13-38

Luke notes carefully all details of the route they follow and the little things in Paul's pastoral concern for his friends. The charge to the elders is moving in simplicity.

Here is the pastoral talk with its courage, humility, frankness. Sorrow, tears, persecutions are recalled. Paul speaks here of "shepherd" (20:18), "elder" (20:17), and "bishop" (20:28) as synonymous terms. His preaching was from house to house (20:20), and bore testimony and witness in personal ways (20:21). He tells of the perils of the ministry; its bonds and afflictions (20:23), and how a man must be "bound in spirit" (20:22) when he purposes a course of action. He wished to finish the course appointed by God (cf. II Tim. 4:7), and he wishes to be free from the blood of all. Is this a boast or a prayer of concern? The Holy Spirit is in his life and in theirs also (20:28).

Yes, Paul "served the Lord with all humility." This can be written into his record. The ministry is spoiled when a man becomes proud in any way or self-centered. We usually know if we are not humble. We cannot tell if we are humble. Others will know the difference. The pompous, noisy, self-assertive person can spoil the witness of the ministry.

Paul sought to "finish the course with joy" (20:24). This he did. He had many scars by the end of the journey. He had been hurt in spirit and mind as well as in body. Nothing moved him from the goal of service for his Lord and Master. He spoke of the pastoral ministry as the one ministry in which he engaged. It meant tears, sacrifice, loneliness, and much toil but in it all the "giving" of himself as he followed the One who spoke of: "it is more blessed to give than to receive."

Acts 21

NO ONE IS FORGOTTEN

21:4. "finding disciples."

21:8. "Philip the evangelist."

21:10. "a certain prophet."

21:16. "an old disciple."

21:28. "This is the man."

I. HISTORICAL SETTING. Paul is now on the journey to Jerusalem and it is attended with interesting happenings. He had left behind him the many churches of Asia Minor and had said good-bye to his friends who did not expect to see him again. Dangers beset his path as there was a mounting opposition wherever his name was mentioned. The word was circulated, evidently, that he was an enemy of Judaism, and thus in all parts his life was in danger. His only safety lay in his right of Roman citizenship. Paul desired to visit Rome as a missionary and meet the church there, but did not know how that would be accomplished. His going to Jerusalem was under the pressure of divine guidance, and yet he knew he went into that city to risk his life. On the way he finds many friends whose names are not to be forgotten before God.

II. EXPOSITORY MEANING. Travel can be interesting because of the scenery enjoyed or it can be memorable because of the people sharing the hours in conversation and fellowship.

Acts 21:4. "Finding disciples." In almost every city or land the Christian can find those of like mind and of like faith. The ever widening circle of friends is part of the richness of Christianity.

Acts 21:4. "Said to Paul through the Spirit." It is strange

how God will speak to us through others. When Christians are given the knowledge of God's will they can assist the individual whose judgment is more limited. Yet there is also the fact that majorities have erred even as church councils have erred. Here Paul was warned by his friends at Tyre. Question their judgment?

Acts 21:5. "With wives and children." It was a touching scene with families involved in the farewell to Paul.

Acts 21:8. "We that were of Paul's company." Check this group for the men with Paul en route. Luke was one.

Acts 21:8. "The house of Philip the evangelist." We meet again one of the Seven Deacons ordained by the church at Jerusalem. Prominent in Chapters 6 and 8, Philip had served the church well. His daughters also shared in serving the church.

Acts 21:10. "A certain prophet." The Twelve were not alone in this distinct title and function. Others were chosen of God.

Acts 21:11. "He [Agabus] took Paul's girdle"—a symbolic act.

Acts 21:12. "Not to go up to Jerusalem." This was the second time this counsel was given (cf. 21:4).

Acts 21:13. "I am ready." The spirit of Paul can be traced in these words here and elsewhere (cf. "I am ready to preach," etc.).

Acts 21:14. "The will of the Lord be done" — not as the last gesture, but should be sought gladly and willingly.

Acts 21:16. "An old disciple." Some who were young in the faith would do well to sit and learn from the experienced.

Acts 21:18. "Went in with us unto James; and all the elders were present." This was a conference of leaders to assess the work done.

Acts 21:19. "He declared particularly what things God had wrought." Paul spoke himself. He *exēgeito* (led out) the details step by step to let the facts speak for themselves. It was through the ministry (*diakonias,* deacon service), not any more than a service anyone else would have done.

Acts 21:20. "Glorified the Lord." It surprised Paul that they rejoiced in the results even as God was praised for it. "Thou seest, brother, how many." This was the language of confidence in and respect for the man who had suffered much.

Acts 21:22. "Multitude must needs come together." They cannot keep this news from the people of Jerusalem.

Acts 21:23-26. These verses describe precautions taken to satisfy the Jews and avoid prejudice.

Acts 21:28. "This is the man." There is no escape from trouble.

Acts 21:36. "Away with him." Here we have a reminder of our Lord's crucifixion.

Acts 21:39. "A citizen of no mean city." Paul is not ashamed of his social and political standing among men.

Acts 21:37, 40. "Canst thou speak [*ginōskeis,* know] Greek? ... He spake in the Hebrew tongue [*dialektō,* dialect]."

III. DOCTRINAL VALUE. In all these changing experiences Paul was conscious of those who stood by him out of every area of the Empire of Rome. Christians rallied to his aid and assisted him again and again. In journeys Paul knew that he was "under orders" and nothing could hinder the work of God through him. All who shared in helping him on his way were partners and fellow-workers. He mentions many in his letters. His friends were legion and came from all walks of life. One of the richest facets of the Christian life is that no one is forgotten who belongs to the fellowship of the church.

IV. PRACTICAL AIM. Encouragement is brought to those who struggle in loneliness and with opposition. Not everyone is "successful" in the life of a disciple, but God will not overlook the faithfulness of those who are loyal and devoted to the faith and to the service of the kingdom of God.

V. HOMILETICAL FORM

Theme: "No One Is Forgotten."

Introduction: The word of God had its way in Europe and Paul now sought to return to Jerusalem to report the victories of the Cross. Many adversaries had opposed; vested interests had hindered; and superstition and bad religion had been a barrier. Yet Paul had witnessed many triumphs of the gospel and was eager to share with the church at Jerusalem. On the way he is showered with love and sympathy, but he knows that he faces trial and death, yet he turns not back. On the way he will remember all his friends who are not forgotten before God.

A. *Disciples at Tyre.* 21:1-6

Paul enjoyed fellowship with these friends and the break in the journey afforded seven days respite. What conversations and confidences; what shared experiences; and what words of Scripture Paul would bring to them. Paul was no tourist on a sight-seeing tour, although he was not insensible to his surroundings. No reference is made to scenery or other events of interest. His chief interest is in people who need the message of the gospel. It is worthwhile to seek out Christians in every city for fellowship.

B. *Philip at Caesarea.* 21:7-9

At the house of the evangelist there would be rejoicing as they talked together about the ministry of the word of God. Philip was not the apostle but one of the seven deacons ordained by the Jerusalem church. At that time Paul was known as Saul and the chief enemy of the infant church. Now Philip entertains the old enemy! His four unmarried daughters were also engaged in a ministry. Woman's place in the church has been discussed from different points of view, but when God gives a woman certain gifts she must exercise them (eg. General William Booth's daughter, the Marechale). Many women have blazed trails of missionary progress across the world.

Paul and Philip together would see the hand of God in their lives and trace divine providence overruling throughout the past. The fellowship of Tyre is now enriched by the hospitality of Caesarea. How rich is Christian fellowship and hospitality! The church is the center of this grace in a way the world outside little knows.

C. *Agabus at Caesarea.* 21:10-14

This prophet is mentioned only here, but his contact with Paul is significant. He sees trouble for Paul, but Paul is not afraid. Note the symbolic act of the prophet as he takes the girdle of Paul. The other Christians seek to dissuade (21:12) even as some had earlier (21:4). They were right in their judgment that trouble lay ahead for Paul, but they were wrong in their interpretation of the trouble. Trial and trouble can face the apostle, but he does not fear this, knowing that God has a purpose in permitting it and would bring him through. Little did these Christians, who thus reasoned, know that Paul's best work and richer ministry was to be as a prisoner at Rome! Paul would be bound, but *the Word of God was not bound.*

Was Paul right in going? Their motive was "love for Paul." His motive in going was "love for Christ." The will of God (21:14) means everything to the Christian who finds it.

D. *Mnason en route.* 21:15-17

This old disciple is one who was that "from the beginning." His faith was rooted far back. He had experience and knowledge beyond many. He is unknown but for this incident. He shelters Paul at this stage. *No one is anonymous with God.* He who receives a prophet receives a prophet's reward. The baggage is packed (21:15) and the journey goes on to the end. We should not forget casual friends sent of God on the way .

E. *Arrival and Arrest.* 21:18-40

Jerusalem at last after the long interval. Three missionary journeys were ended and much done for Christ. Was the church unfriendly at first? His report to the church is striking and the response gratifying. He agrees to retain ritual for the sake of his brethren. This, after he had risked his life abroad! But humbly he submits. His compromise did not necessarily help him finally. The Temple he entered was now without its Messiah and would fall. The mob attacks and anarchy reigns for a little, and Paul is counted as an anarchist, a lawless one! So is prejudice, blindness, and passion when they sway the crowd. Difficult now to secure "rights," hence the arrest and imprisonment.

The final picture is Paul self-controlled and ready for his defense. "Can you speak [do you know] Greek?" The use of the Hebrew dialect in reply startles the soldier in charge of his prisoner. Paul did not say he was a Christian here, but claimed his freedom for trial as a Roman citizen. Political rights may be used for the gospel. "Greek . . . Hebrew" — the languages of both culture and religion, of Hellenism and Hebraism. These are the bases of our evangelism today. We speak of a message whose content is rooted in the past, but we proclaim and communicate in the language of our day.

Even as the Lord has raised up many friends for Paul and none is forgotten before God, so He will stand by His servant now in the day of the ordeal.

Acts 22

DEFENDING THE CHRISTIAN FAITH

22:1. "Hear ye my defense."

22:2. "When they heard . . . the Hebrew tongue . . . they kept . . . silence."

22:3, 25, 26, 28. "I . . . am a Jew . . . a man . . . a Roman . . . freeborn."

I. HISTORICAL SETTING. Paul's return to Jerusalem to bring a report of his journeys to the church there was satisfactory in that respect. However, when his enemies learned he was in the city they pressed for his arrest and condemnation. A short respite is given him as he claims his rights to speak as a citizen of Rome.

II. EXPOSITORY MEANING. The details of Paul's speech carry some duplication of his earlier account of his conversion. This time he is not only testifying, but also using the way of the apology or defense in argument.

Acts 22:1. "Men, brethren, and fathers." This made good contact— was conciliatory.

Acts 22:1. "Hear ye my defense." The defense *(apologias)* is better described as the Apologia.

Acts 22:2. "When they heard . . . Hebrew tongue . . . they kept silence." Language and dialect can either please or widen the breach. Paul's dialect quieted them and they became silent and ready to listen.

Acts 22:3. "I am . . . a Jew . . . brought up . . . at the feet of Gamaliel." A full statement of background, education, and religion is in this verse. His status is unquestioned, and he can remind them that in zeal he is no different than they.

Acts 22:4. "I persecuted this way." Paul confesses the best and worst together. He pleases former friends: acknowledges his sin in the light of new friends. Emphatic — "This Way" — refers to the new Way in Christ, the people of The Way.

Acts 22:6, 9, 11. "A great light . . . the light . . . the glory of that light." That light was greater than sunshine? Now we know about the light of atomic energy when exploded.

Acts 22:9. "Saw the light, but heard not the voice." The voice was for Saul, personally.

Acts 22:14. "The God of our fathers hath chosen [pro-exeirisato — choice is that of election?] thee to know his will." This is the significant knowledge for the Christian.

Acts 22:15. "Thou shalt be his witness (martus)." Paul is a martyr for the faith.

Acts 22:21. "I will send thee far hence." Little did he think of how far reaching this would be!

Acts 22:24. "Examined for scourging." This was the customary prelude to crucifixion. Paul was walking in the steps of his Master and Lord.

Acts 22:26, 28. "A Roman . . . great sum bought freedom . . . freeborn." This has reference to his political status (politeian).

III. DOCTRINAL VALUE. The Christian faith shines out when under scrutiny and trial. Paul's repeated story of his conversion is part of Christian evidences. When men seek or demand proof concerning the rights of Christianity this is one method by which men can see what Christianity can do. The realm of the experimental is an effective way to convince the unbeliever. Christianity works, and it works by changing lives, such as Saul's.

IV. PRACTICAL AIM. In the proclamation of the gospel it is not enough to expound propositions of truth. We need to illustrate them by examples of transformed lives. The church should be able to point to people who are the living witnesses of the truth proclaimed. Conversions and converts are potent items in the arsenal of truth. The weapons of our warfare are spiritual, and the spiritual miracles of new creations in Christ is one of the best means of apologetic preaching.

V. HOMILETICAL FORM:

Theme: "Defending the Christian Faith."

Introduction: There are times when the church must defend what it believes. Generally the church proclaims its belief by preaching and teaching, but there are occasions when attacked that the church must give evidence to prove its claims. This is not an easy method, yet it has its place. Every age has demanded some proof and there are agnostics, atheists, and unbelievers of all kinds who refuse to listen except on the basis of evidence or a proof of power outside of themselves.

The old forms of apologetics have passed away. We are not confronted today with much of Deism as in the 18th century, or of Atheism and Agnosticism as in the 19th century. But other forms of attack against Christianity have emerged in Communism and its dialectical materialism; also there is the challenge of a skeptical science which would eliminate God from our universe. Other phases of attack center in the Bible as well as in the person of Christ. The Church must have a reason for its hope and be ready to combat the forces arrayed against it. We need apologetic preaching and teaching and writing today. Paul used the Apologia to witness.

A. *The Opportunity.* 22:1-21

Because of his use of Hebrew and Greek languages, Paul was in a good position when challenged.

(1) Contact was easy (22:1-2). He was conciliatory, friendly, respectful. His speech enlisted sympathetic hearing. Paul was in chains, yet he was noble in bearing. The Hebrew dialect was a good channel of communication. The vernacular tongue for any man is effective. Luther in Germany; Wyclif in England; and the various translations and versions have made the Bible a book to be read and received.

(2) Conversion was unforgettable (22:3-14). As in Chapter 9 (and later in Chapter 26) Paul does not tire of telling the story. Christian experience of the spiritual life is worth repeating. Paul, and other preachers, since have found that preaching is most telling when there is woven into it the

personal testimony of what Christ has done. In the details of this story Paul never lost the glow and the wonder of that birth-hour of the Spirit.

(3) Consecration was balanced (22:15-21). All that was mentioned came as the outflow of the new life in Christ. The new man lives a new life. Paul declares that his public alliance with God's people in the church helped him to live down some of his dark past and helped to show he was now a Christian. He claimed to be commissioned by the risen Lord. In the will of God for his life he had found the work to do.

B. *The Opposition.* 22:22-30

The highway to Damascus was the scene of the conversion of Paul, but he had to travel also the highway of misunderstanding and insult to Jerusalem. Past sins rose up to haunt him and embarrass him.

(1) The Attack against him (22:22-25). The mob out of hand is dangerous. As a servant of Christ Paul now shares a little of what his Master endured. "Away with him!" is familiar, as Paul must have heard that when Jesus was led away to the Cross. "Scourging" was a prelude to condemnation and the test most severe. Today's brainwashing and physical and mental cruelties in communistic imprisonments are in line with the worst evil. Paul found exemption from scourging by his defense of "rights."

(2) The Appeal of Paul (22:26-30). His defense is clear. He stands by the rights of Roman citizenship. Some Christians have been martyred to death and have lost all rights and that is the risk of being a missionary in enemy territory. The Boxer Rising in China and the brutalities in the Congo are reminders of this. Here Paul wisely uses what is legitimate as an expediency. As "free-born" he claimed the natural rights in order to advance the spiritual rights of the gospel.

The defense of the Christian faith continues everywhere. Paul has given a clear picture of how the truth must be defended. Reasoned debate and clear thinking are part of the method. There will be simple testimony and honest exposition of the Scriptures of truth, but there is room for apologetic words. This is not apologizing for what we believe, but setting a defense for the sake of the gospel.

The languages used by Paul are indicative of the need of educated men to defend the gospel. Others can witness by the simple word, an honest character, and the radiant spirit. But sometimes we need the man specially fitted for this other task. Scholars with knowledge of languages, archaeology, and other gifts of mind and character are given a place in the over-all defense of the gospel. The Hebrew tongue brings us knowledge first-hand of the Old Testament Scriptures which are the foundation of all the promises to be fulfilled in Christ. The Greek of the New Testament is the one vehicle by which God providentially spread the gospel through the Roman Empire in the first century. To those who claim their belief in the whole Bible as the Word of God, fully inspired of God, it is not too much to ask that the exponents of the gospel should have some acquaintance with and use of the original languages of the Bible. We make our best defense of the truth of the gospel when we silence our enemies with the power of a changed life, but it helps to convince some when we can use the other qualifications of life, whether educational, political, social, or national. Every contact for Christ is usable by him.

Acts 23

A CHRISTIAN CONSCIENCE

23:1. "I have lived in all good conscience before God."

23:5. "I wist not brethren, that he was the high priest."

23:9. "We find no evil in this man."

Cf. 24:16. *"herein do I exercise myself to have always a conscience void of offense toward God, and man."*

I. HISTORICAL SETTING. Paul under arrest is finally brought to appear before the council of the Jews. Roman authorities seek a just trial for him. The leadership of Judaism is present for this occasion. All are prejudiced and Paul is prejudged in this trial. Charges are made against him and these he must refute. Sometimes circumstantial evidence is against him in the semblance of truth, and again truth is with him implicitly.

II. EXPOSITORY MEANING. The interplay of this trial brings out the inner motives and attitudes of the Apostle. He cannot argue beyond his conscience, the guide for this occasion and exercised by the Holy Spirit.

Acts 23:1. "I have lived in all good conscience." His life in the past was directed in this light. His actions recently, as a Christian, have also been motivated accordingly. The conscience *(suneidēsei)* is important.

Acts 23:2. "To smite him on the mouth." Brutal treatment is part of regimes where Christ is rejected. Evil finds physical sadism part of its method of warfare, then and now.

Acts 23:3. "Whited wall." This is a term of derision and a judgment of condition (cf. sepulchre-painted white?)

Acts 23:5. "I wist not, brethren, that he was the high priest." Paul stood corrected and humbly apologizes for his mistaken judgment. Was Paul suffering from eye trouble that he did not see clearly?

Acts 23:6. "I am called in question." Paul's clever strategy is to divide the two parties present: Sadducees and Pharisees — naturalism and supernaturalism; liberal and conservative.

Acts 23:12. "Bound themselves... until they had killed Paul." Here we have conspiracy and vendetta to get rid of Paul. Man's evil desire is here expressed.

Acts 23:16. "Paul's sister's son." God uses an unnamed young man to be an instrument to save Paul's life. Paul had no human help thus far in the trial.

Acts 23:29. "Questions of their law, but to have nothing laid to his charge worthy of death or of bonds." Impartial Roman justice could sift out the real issues at stake.

III. DOCTRINAL VALUE. The conscience of the Christian is an important factor in the basic issues of life. This is one of the ways in which God guides the Christian. How it operates and how it brings moral issues to their ultimate end in judgment is not always easy to determine. Whether the mind or the emotions plays the larger part is not resolved. Perhaps the total personality is charged with a moral sense in knowing what is the right which should be followed. Conscience is enlightened for the Christian and the light shining upon his conscience is more powerful than that which shines upon an ordinary man.

IV. PRACTICAL AIM. This shows that Paul as a man knew fear and anxiety when under pressure. He did not always behave as an exemplary Christian. He made mistakes and knew embarrassment when wrong. Yet the bent and direction of his life was motivated by a good conscience at all times. The Christian needs to cultivate the conscience. There is that which is beyond the judgment of wrong and right; there is the better and the best.

V. HOMILETICAL FORM

Theme: "A Christian Conscience."

Introduction: Paul in his letters has much to say about the inner life of the Christian. He is not a psychologist as moderns think of one, but he had psychological insight far beyond others of his day. He dealt with the Christian life in basic terms, ever seeking to stimulate the person to higher living under God. He probes and stabs; he unveils and directs; he shows knowledge of the heart of man in its temptation, fears, aspirations, prayers, trials and overcoming. Paul was a master of the mind of man and knew what was in man's mind. To achieve a sound mind and a right balanced life, Paul could testify about a clear conscience, a Christian conscience.

A. *Conscience is not infallible.* 23:1-5

Paul could make a mistake in judgment. At his trial he was angry against the presiding officer of the council. He did not realize that this man was the High Priest. He cited him as "whited wall" — a term of contempt and disdain. When Paul found out that he had said this about the Jewish leader, he apologized as he knew it was wrong to speak thus against God's officer.

The court procedures allowed Paul to speak which was helpful. He had a passion for the right. Compared by any other standard of behavior Paul was strong and sublime in what he did and said, but in the light of Christ's trial what is the judgment? "When Christ was reviled, He reviled not again"; but when Paul was reviled? there is the difference.

This self-knowledge of the individual is striking. It is a distinguishing feature in man. Man perceives good and bad, right and wrong. This principle of reflection leads man to approve or disapprove his actions. It is a judgment, not merely of fact, but upon fact. It's language is not "I like," but "I ought." Certainly this has been given by God to the soul, and in the deepest sense it is what we are, in ourselves, before God.

B. *Conscience is active.* 23:6-16

Paul's insight to weigh up a situation is noted here. He is shrewd when he perceives that two religious groups represent the Council before whom he appears on trial. Paul then divides the Council theologically on their basic beliefs. He is on one side, because, as a Pharisee in background and now as a Christian, he wholeheartedly believes in the supernatural — i.e. the Resurrection and all that is attendant upon

the life unseen. Thus he gains sympathy and support in the
Council. He had no human resources to help him in this
trial. Paul's crime was that he insisted that Christ was universal in his supremacy or else Christ was no Messiah at all.
That is the crux of the trial and the Jewish proverb had it,
"the secret of man is the secret of the Messiah."

In Paul's defense there was dissension that followed his
talk. The soldiers were ready to "protect him" (23:10) ; the
Lord's presence was insufficient to "cheer" him (23:11) ;
but no church group was there to pray for him it seems.
Lonely and tired after two days trial, the enemies of Paul
attack again and the "oath to slay him" is taken (23:12-16).
Paul is the forerunner of many others in prison (Luther at
Wartburg; Rutherford at Aberdeen; Bunyan at Bedford).

Some of Paul's acts seem strange and may be questioned,
but the conscience is guide. It is active and working. He
could claim it to have been "good" (23:1) ; and "void of
offense" (24:16). It was not seared, evil, weak, or defiled.
Later he writes to Timothy about a "pure" conscience
(I Tim. 3:9; II Tim. 1:3). This could be his state of conscience in the trial as he rebutted his enemies and endeavored
by every known human way to escape death.

C. *Conscience is Demanding.* 23:16-35

Whatever Paul said or did, he would not escape the implications of his acts and decisions. If he should be imprisoned, he would have time to reflect. If committed to
death or if murdered, the end had come. But Paul knew
that he still wished to see Rome and he had certain rights
as a Roman citizen, and perhaps he would find a way of escape
yet.

The tale is romantic in its way of deliverance for Paul.
There is no thunder, no lightening, no miraculous escape
(like Peter from prison, cf. Acts 11-12). God here works
through human channels. He prompts the youth, he arranges
for a guard of soldiers, and 470 escort Paul safely! The
natural means are the ways of the supernatural in providence.
God works with details and the seemingly trivial in life are
not unimportant. The Almighty God is the all-methodical

God and He is on the field of battle even when invisible. Paul had been loyal to truth and never sacrificed principle. The mob might rage and demand his blood, but the man of God is sure of the outcome.

Paul had a clear conscience. It was a Christian conscience. Differences there are and will be in the expressions of Christians' actions. Variations will be noted between God's people. Each will speak of obeying conscience. Whence these differences? It depends upon the light which shines upon the conscience. Some have greater light, clearer light; others have twi-light. Roman moralists followed the law of nature; devout Jews lived according to the Mosaic Law; but the Christian lives by the Spirit of Christ and the Word of God operating upon his conscience.

Some will have fuller knowledge than others, and a few will find conscience more sensitive than others. Later, Paul will confess "I verily thought within myself that *I ought to do* many things contrary to the name of Jesus Christ" (Acts 26:9). In this he looked back to his pre-Christian days. Beyond that in the new life he could testify that his conscience as a Christian was clear. The demand made upon him was that of cleansing of the conscience (Heb. 9:14; 10:2, 22). After that cleansing and purging by Christ came the quiet, steady habit of *exercising* the conscience. It was alert and awake, ever bringing him to judgment before Christ.

Acts 24

WHEN LAW AND GOSPEL CONFLICT

24:1. "Ananias the high priest."

24:1. "A certain orator ... Tertullus."

24:6. "Judged according to our law."

24:21. "Touching the resurrection of the dead I am called in question by you this day."

24:22. "when Felix heard these things, having more perfect knowledge of THE WAY, he deferred them."

24:25. "As he reasoned of righteousness, temperance, and judgment to come, Felix trembled, and answered, Go thy way for this time."

I. HISTORICAL SETTING. Paul before Felix is preceded in the debate with the orator Tertullus who represented the High Priest and the legal forces arrayed against him. He had been passed from the Jerusalem court to the court at Caesarea. Ananias came down from Jerusalem and still prosecuted the charge against Paul. There is no doubt that the Jewish leader understood that if Paul was not stopped now, Christianity would have a new lease of power and outreach across the world. It was in this tense atmosphere of spleen and anger when Paul stood trial again.

II. EXPOSITORY MEANING. Here we trace the battle of words in the struggle for religious freedom. The battle of the mind is always present when men are in tension concerning the law and the gospel.

Acts 24:1. "A certain orator ... Tertullus." He had been engaged by the authorities in Jerusalem to prosecute this case. He was a Roman lawyer, obviously, who had that advantage in the courts.

134

Acts 24:2. "Began to accuse him ... Seeing that by thee we enjoy great quietness" — contrasted words and ideas: the first to state the case against the prisoner, the second to gain the ear of the bench.

Acts 24:3. "Most noble Felix" — his excellency.

Acts 24:4. "I pray thee" — courtesy in address, making humble plea.

Acts 24:5. "Pestilent fellow ... mover of sedition ... ringleader of the sect of the Nazarenes." This is a blacklist against Paul. Name-calling can be bad. Unconsciously testimony to truth is often in these charges, and not always the way intended by the accusers.

Acts 24:6. "We ... would have judged according to our law." That would have been biased in this case and unjust. Thanks to Roman law Paul was given this open trial.

Acts 24:10. "I do the more cheerfully answer." Spirit and passion are here involved, not joy or gladness.

Acts 24:13. "Neither can they prove the things."

Acts 24:14. "But this I confess ... after THE WAY." Paul's willing confession of certain facts brings out the heart of the problem.

Acts 24:11, 14. "Went ... to ... worship ... so worship" (latreuō).

Acts 24:14. "Believing all things ... written in the law and in the prophets" — a believer in the writings of the Old Testament.

Acts 24:15. "There shall be a resurrection of the dead" (cf. 24:21. "Touching the resurrection of the dead, I am called in question."). This was the judgment — Paul's testimony to the resurrection.

Acts 24:22. "Felix ... more perfect knowledge" — more accurate knowledge of THE WAY.

Acts 24:25. "Reasoned of righteousness, temperance, and judgment to come" — three issues inescapable.

Acts 24:25. "Felix trembled." He was afraid. Fear is an important influence in life to move the will.

Acts 24:25. More "convenient season."

Acts 24:26. "Hoped money should have been given."
Bribery — a wrong motive to listen to the gospel.

III. DOCTRINAL VALUE. Shows that the Law has its
limitations. The Old Testament Law and the law expounded
by Rome and Judaism together tried to condemn Paul. The
spirit of the law was an end in death. The gospel, in contrast,
brought life from the dead. It centered in the fact of resurrection and set free from condemnation.

IV. PRACTICAL AIM. When the gospel is proclaimed to
a crowd or as here to one individual there is the need for
directness and appeal for decision. Paul pleaded for the soul
of this Roman governor in vain. The man had mixed motives and was not open in mind and heart to receive the
truth whatever it cost. The gospel must deal with righteousness, self-control, and judgment to come.

V. HOMILETICAL FORM
Theme: "When Law and Gospel Conflict."
Introduction: This is a striking and thrilling occasion
when Paul was faced with the charges against his faith. The
religious leaders employed one of the best minds to present
their case in an attempt to catch Paul. But here Paul is seen
as a man with a clear-cut, definite confession of faith which
cannot be shaken. He also uses the opportunity to defend
himself and proclaim the gospel to those who will listen to
him.

A. *The Law's Demands.* 24:1-9
Paul is standing in Herod's judgment hall before Felix
and a letter is brought in with the charge against him. His
reception is not promising.

(1) The Accusation (24:1a) reveals the enmity of the
High Priest, Ananias, who had travelled rapidly to get there.
He was probably an old man, but still active in intrigue.

(2) The Impeachment of the Orator (24:1b-9). He had
been "briefed" for this trial. Tertullus, a Roman lawyer, had
a fee to earn, especially if he won the case. With wile and
flattery he appealed to the emotions and not to facts. He
began his speech, not with the case, but with a eulogy of the

governor! Note the "peace we enjoy" — yet they had just
had tumult and disorder! In the charge against Paul he said
"this pestilent fellow" — "sect of the Nazarenes" etc., but
never "a disciple of Jesus the Christ." Was it planned that
way to blot out the name of Jesus? As far as they were concerned Jesus was officially dead and out of the way! Here
was the "smear" tactics and the prejudice against Paul used
cleverly.

Paul had been charged with; plotted against in Damascus;
at Jerusalem; expelled from Pisidian Antioch; stoned at
Lystra; scourged and imprisoned at Philippi; accused of
treason at Thessalonica; charged as causing a riot at Ephesus; and now with rioting at Jerusalem! No wonder it was
said that the early Christians "turned the world upside
down."

Paul could not deny the essence of these events, although
he was not guilty of evil intent and deliberate planning so
to do.

B. *The Apostle's Defense.* 24:10-21

See Paul standing alone without any help.

(1) Beginning of his rebuttal. Paul is courteous and conciliatory in a difficult situation. Courtesy is not flattery (as
in the case of Tertullus). Paul was an able man with a clear
and nimble mind. "I answer for myself."

No attorney-lawyer is here to speak for him, but the Holy
Spirit, the Paraclete, the Advocate, is there to help him.

(2) Appeals to Felix. Paul states the case logically and
faces the issues clearly. He denies the charges and demands
proof. Those who accuse (the real accusers) should present
themselves to prove their case. This is in accord with Roman
law, but those people are absent.

(3) Confesses "the Way which they call heresy." This is
the heart of the matter. It concerns THE WAY. This new
way of life in Christ challenges entrenched evil and religious
vested interests. It cannot do otherwise as it brings the
dynamic of the resurrection in the living Christ.

C. *The Gospel's Decision.* 24:22-27

The result in court gave Paul victory in his argument and

he should have been set free, but policy and expediency
resulted in vacillation and compromise. It was Pilate with
Jesus over again in principle.

(1) Delay the case and judgment (24:22-23). Felix as
judge played politics and sought his own ends selfishly.

(2) Delay the Christian decision (24:24-27). Felix as a
man before God, procrastinated. Note Paul's sermon or talk
on righteousness, self-control, and judgment to come. Compare the work of the Holy Spirit (John 16:8) as an Advocate
coming to convince the conscience of sin, righteousness, and
judgment and the reasons given: of sin, because of unbelief;
of righteousness, because of the ascension; and of judgment,
because the prince of this world is judged. That work of
reproof or convicting was now demonstrated in the case of
Felix. He was aware of these truths as they affected him personally. He was afraid and in that emotion sought release,
not by repentance but by compromise. He procrastinated;
he listened to the evil women by his side; he avariciously
thought of what money he could gain; and thus he played
with the claims of Christ for two years and made no decision.
The "faith in Christ" (24:24) demands a verdict.

Thus the Law of Judaism could not bring salvation but
became a means to point up the need for the gospel. The law
of Rome could not bring truth to light but became a means
to stifle truth because of the corruption of men's hearts. It
was the gospel alone which brought the truth to light and
offered the fulness of life to those who would believe and
receive.

Acts 25

SEPARATION OF CHURCH AND STATE

25:11. "I appeal unto Caesar."

25:19. "certain questions . . . of their own superstition."

I. HISTORICAL SETTING. Paul is passed from one court to another before he reaches the final tribunal. From Jerusalem he has gone to Caesarea and now at Caesarea he will be returned to Jerusalem unless a decision is made to send him to Rome. He has been before Felix and now he appears before Festus and also Agrippa. These governors and petty kings maintained their courts and exercised Roman law in the far flung empire of their Caesar. Except that Paul claimed his rights as a Roman citizen, he would have been forgotten long ago.

II. EXPOSITORY MEANING
Acts 25:1. "Festus ascended from Caesarea to Jerusalem." Cf. 24:1 — where Ananias "descended" from Jerusalem to Caesarea. The capital city has precedence in position and respect.

Acts 25:3. "Lying in wait in the way to kill him." If Paul had been sent by Festus to Jerusalem the plot to kill him would have been attempted. Did Festus see through the scheming and conniving of the High Priest and so refuse?

Acts 25:5. "Let them . . . able . . . go down . . . accuse this man, if . . ." Festus evidently knew what had transpired under Felix. Now he calls the bluff of the Jews in fine satire.

Acts 25:7. "Complaints against Paul, which they could not prove." No facts were produced, only innuendoes.

Acts 25:10, 11, 12. "I stand at Caesar's judgment seat . . . I appeal unto Caesar . . . Hast thou appealed unto Caesar? unto Caesar shalt thou go." History was made that day when

Paul claimed his rights of citizenship. Political ideals have certain influence for the Christian.

Acts 25:16. "Not the manner of the Romans to deliver any man to die." Roman justice demanded that there be a face to face trial of accusers and the tried.

Acts 25:18. "Brought none accusation of such things as I supposed." As a judge, Festus could sift evidence clearly.

Acts 25:19. "But had certain questions against him of their own superstition, and of one Jesus." *Deisidaimonias,* the Roman idea of religion as another matter of the demonic powers. By adding "one Jesus" the true issue was introduced. Again, the risen Christ is the crucial fact of Christianity.

Acts 25:26, 27. "That, after examination had, I might have somewhat to write. For it seemeth to me unreasonable to send a prisoner, and not signify the crimes against him." Here is fairplay of the Roman mind seeking to be just in every detail.

III. DOCTRINAL VALUE. Our Lord had laid down the principle that the Christian should "render to Caesar the things that are Caesar's; and to God, the things that are God's" (Matt. 22:21). The truth is nowhere more explicit than under the government of the Roman powers whereby the Christian church had to live. This government was a dictatorship, yet by seeking to obey this truth they were guaranteed certain rights. Not all Christians were citizens as Paul, and he could use his political franchise for the sake of the gospel.

IV. PRACTICAL AIM. To show that a Christian need not succumb to the first demands of the state. What is legitimate and right for the people of the state, should be used by the Christian church. We do not control the state and the state cannot control the church. Separation of church and state is a good thing. Let this be changed and there is trouble. The church must be free to act as the conscience of the state and be able to speak to the state what is right in the sight of God. The state is of divine institution and government must be respected. The Christian must decide his relation to both state and to God.

V. HOMILETICAL FORM

Theme: "Separation of Church and State."

Introduction: This is a crucial issue in our day. When Paul lived under the Roman Empire he lived under totalitarianism. The Caesar had all-power. However, certain rights and privileges were granted to those who were citizens. The Jews, like other subject people, did not have the same rights. The Christian church composed of many backgrounds also stood in the same unenviable position. Yet some of the Christians, like Paul, had political freedom and could use this for the sake of the gospel. Paul in his contacts with Roman authorities brings us guidance concerning our attitudes for modern days of unrest.

A. *The Governor.* 25:1-5

The man appointed under God to govern is one who should have respect and honor. Festus here was not a man of strong character. Felix was weak and vacillating (cf. Acts 24). He had been a slave before rising to power. He was cruel and unjust; a slave to his passions. Festus was an anaemic character with indecision. His administration was mixed with curiosity and ignorance concerning Paul and the Christian faith. He was a worldling and the natural man cannot see the spiritual realm.

The Jews were still hostile after two years and Festus was open to their pleas, but he did see through duplicity. He was not easily coerced by Paul's enemies and was suspicious of their judgment. However, he appears to be non-committal and indecisive. Paul in his Roman letter speaks of paying tribute as well as respect to those in office (cf. Romans 13). We may not have high regard for some men in political office, but if they are there, the Christian must respect the office if he cannot always endorse the incumbent of that office. This is not easy, for it includes that we pray for those in office (cf. I Tim. 2).

B. *The Government.* 25:6-14.

We expect from good government the just decisions in court and the freedoms for human life and dignity which go with our traditional heritage. But what of those who lived under totalitarianism? Paul endured that.

Government here begins honestly and with fairness. Paul's enemies state their case and this time there is no Roman lawyer-orator! Paul defends himself and Festus made a compromise. He would gratify the Jews. He would not change the venue, but he shirks duty in this case. Policy and not principle (25:10) operate again. He consults the Council. He shifts responsibility finally by seeking Agrippa to decide (25:13-14). If Festus refuses to acquit Paul, then he must formulate a charge against him to send him to Rome.

We expect from government *justice*. Roman law was noted for this spirit of equity and honesty. No Roman could be tried without a fair hearing. Others might not receive the same treatment, but the politically free were entitled to this. Roman law and justice was known throughout the world. Paul as a representative of the Christian church could not only claim freedom of speech and liberty of action, but he could also challenge the actions of government when those actions conflicted with the supreme truth of God. God was "Lord of the conscience."

C. *The Governed.* 25:15-27

Paul, the representative Christian, finds opportunity to witness concerning the Faith. Even Festus has to admit that the charge against Paul is unreliable without any facts to prove it. The main quarrel and the crux of everything finally is Christianity. If Christ is alive as Paul claims, then something has happened in the world to change all life.

Here is the crux in our day. Christians live in the state as loyal citizens, but there could be occasions when their faith is in tension with demands of the state. What if the state were dominated by religious despotism? What if the state controlled religious institutions and leaders? These are alternative dangers ever present. They have arisen in other lands and in other times, but what if they should come to us in the new world?

The glamour and pomp of royalty is expressed in king Agrippa with Bernice, coming to listen to Paul speak.

Agrippa as a former Jew knew much about the new WAY. His great-grandfather killed the Bethlehem children; his grand-uncle killed John the Baptist; his father killed James and imprisoned Peter; and each of his relatives passed to an untimely death. He knew that the destiny of the house of Agrippa was connected with Christ and their attitude to Him. What new thing could this prisoner, Paul, have to say to him? There was one thing. He would find out (cf. Acts 26).

Paul had appealed to Caesar. Right or wrong, when the Jews violated justice and broke their law, he turned to the government of Rome to maintain law. He would be "subject to the higher powers" (Rom. 13:1). In this court, the prisoner is greater than the governor.

Politics are the means of a Christian exercising his freedom and franchise of citizenship. We tender to Caesar not only taxes, but take responsibility for good government. We pray for those in authority. We obey as long as conscience allows. God is first. Normal life in a state should bring opportunities to advance the gospel, the message of the living Christ who reigns over all governments.

Acts 26

ALMOST OR ALTOGETHER A CHRISTIAN?

26:29. "I would to God, that not only thou, but also all that hear me this day, were both almost, and altogether such as I am, except these bonds."

I. HISTORICAL SETTING. The last of the many trials of Paul before going to Rome find him before King Agrippa. The king has been called in by Festus to assist in the decision and judgment concerning Paul's appeal to Caesar. Again Paul makes an apologia or defense as he tells his story and pleads his cause. The court scene is striking with the guards around; the judgment seat of Agrippa; the woman accompanying him; the purple and scarlet of the courtiers; and, in contrast, the prisoner in chains.

II. EXPOSITORY MEANING. In the tension of opposing points of view we hear the principal men speak. Sometimes one word gives them away.

Acts 26:1. "Permitted to speak for thyself" — given open way to speak on your behalf, *huper.*

Acts 26:2. "I shall answer for myself." *peri,* concerning.

Acts 26:3. "Expert in all customs and questions which are among the Jews." *gnōstēn,* the one who knows.

Acts 26:8. "Why...incredible...God should raise the dead?" This was something beyond faith.

Acts 26:9. "I...thought with myself." It seemed to me. We can be mistaken and think in wrong way. "I ought to do ...contrary to the name of Jesus." "To do," *praxai,* is imperative not always for the right.

Acts 26:10. "I gave my voice against them." Note the ways in which voting was done.

Acts 26:11. "Exceedingly mad against them." Paul's early zeal in religion brought hatred, not love — a state of mind in which reason was not in control.

Acts 26:14. "To kick against the pricks" — goad of the sharp point used to urge forward cattle.

Acts 26:16. "I have appeared unto thee for this purpose ... to make thee a minister and a witness," *hupēretēn,* under-rower.

Acts 26:18. "To open their eyes and to turn them from darkness" — spiritual enlightenment and convert them from the authority of Satan and an inheritance, rich deposit — among the set apart ones, the saints.

Acts 26:22. "Witnessing both to small and great" — people of all walks of life, and now the "great" — before kings.

Acts 26:22. "Those which the prophets and Moses did say should come." Paul accepted the sacred writings of the Old Testament. They were filled with Messianic promise and hope.

Acts 26:23. "Christ should suffer, and ... rise from the dead." The twin facts of redemption — sufferings and glory.

Acts 26:24. "Festus said ... thou art beside thyself; much learning doth make thee mad." "Learning" — *grammata,* letters.

Acts 26:28. "Almost ... persuadest me to be a Christian." How did he say this? Credulous? Sneering? Jocular? It is difficult to interpret without the tone of voice and gesture. Possibly a grain of sincerity in it in the light of Paul's reply.

Acts 26:29. "Both almost, and altogether such as I am, except these bonds." This is the strength of Paul's gospel. He desires him for Christ, but would not impose the chain of the prisoner.

III. DOCTRINAL VALUE. To fix attention upon the teaching about a Christian. What is a Christian? Agrippa asked a question and made a statement of purpose with reference to this all-embracing word. There was an idea behind it; a knowledge of content; a meaning given. What then can we learn about a Christian from Paul? Three times the word is used in the New Testament and each has its own contribution. Here a Christian is one who seeks the best for an enemy, without the chain of punishment and imprisonment.

IV. PRACTICAL AIM. Witnessing for Christ brings out the nature of the Christian faith and the spirit of the Christian life. In this hour Paul's earnest desire to win Agrippa to be a Christian heightened the scope of evangelism. The end of our service in the church is not to add numbers to our rolls, but to bring people into a new life wherein they develop into the likeness of Christ.

V. HOMILETICAL FORM

Theme: "Almost or Altogether a Christian?"

Introduction: When the gospel is proclaimed there are responses of various kinds. Some people are ready to receive the truth in obedience and others are not ready to accept anything which would disrupt their lives. At the trial of Paul, Festus, Agrippa, and Bernice were present and each gave away the point of view in one word. Festus said to Paul "mad!" He was an interrupter and one who did not understand the simple things of which Paul talked. Agrippa said: almost you persuade me. He was interested but not committed or convinced. Bernice listened and said nothing but in her attitude revealed indifference and opposition. What difference is there in being almost or altogether?

A. *The Interrupter Festus.*

All through the contacts with Paul he had had an opportunity to know more about the Christian faith. His mind was not vitally concerned. He sought favor with the Jews (25:9a) ; he wished to stand well with Agrippa (25:14) ; he sought fair play and justice at first (25:25-37) ; but finally he had a conscience stifled (26:24). That one word "mad" gave him away. Paul had spoken about "visions, revelation, voices, resurrection" — these pointed to a mind unbalanced, although Paul had the sound mind and Festus unbalanced! It all seemed foolish to Festus.

Paul had been "mad" once against Christians, but now Festus will charge he is "mad," because of enthusiasm. The natural man cannot understand the things of the Spirit, and therefore insulates himself from the blessing. He fails to realize that passion is not madness, and only spiritual passion counts in Christian witness.

B. *The Indifferent Bernice.*

This woman by the side of Agrippa is a spectator on

the side-line. "Agrippa . . . *and* Bernice with great pomp"
(25:23) indicate what is there. "Agrippa rose up . . . *and*
Bernice" (26:30) reveal that they were partners in life and
decisions. They withdrew and spoke together, so that her
influence was strong over the king. Bernice is silent, and so
is Scripture silent. An immoral woman, sister of king Agrippa, with glitter, glamour, and court glory — these meant more
to her than the reality of the Christian appeal. Often one like
this will hinder a decisive action for Christ.

C. *The Interested Agrippa.*

An unprincipled man, yet he could be gracious (26:1).
He gave Paul liberty to speak. He knew much of the background (26:26, 27). Agrippa was impressed as Paul spoke
and challenged him. With truth and soberness the king was
persuaded and moved, ready to act. "Would you fain make
me a Christian?" Either earnest and sincere, or flippant and
trifling. Yet verses 30-32 point to tragedy as he turns aside
finally from that decisive act of committal.

Remember Paul's message in verses 16-18 treats of the
consequences of committal. The tragic word then is "almost."
The runner almost reaches the post; the ship almost gains
the harbor; the marksman almost hits the target. As the owl
peeps at the sun out of the barn, but does not come out to
enjoy it; so men like Agrippa peep at Christianity, winking
and blinking as though afraid. Self-love; the fear of man; the
ties of immoral conduct; these hinder a man who *knows* the
truth yet trifles at his peril.

D. *The Invincible Paul.*

Physically he did not impress. His appeal in speech to
Agrippa lay in its sincerity and passion. His spirit transformed him as he pleaded with the soul of a man. His witness came out of experience and conversion. That was real.
"I would to God you could be as I am . . . except these
bonds." That is Christianity at white heat. That is the heart
of the missionary evangelist. That is the message of the New
Testament. Once Paul, many years before, had persecuted
the people of the Way: now he would willingly give his own
life to save an Agrippa. He would give the privileges, but

not the burdens and sufferings. He would offer the freedom and not the chains. The sincerity of a religious zeal that persecutes is not Christian: the sincerity now that would die to save and deliver a man but will not add a chain is Christian.

The vital distinction then is between "almost" and "altogether." Those like Agrippa who are near but not all the way; who are almost but not altogether; these remain on the outside and miss the inner knowledge of conversion. Those like Paul who are "altogether," wholly committed are found with the people of the Way who know and know that they know.

Acts 27

CRISIS AND CONFIDENCE

27:15. "And when the ship was caught, and could not bear up into the wind, we let her drive."

27:22. "Be of good cheer: for there shall be no loss of ... life among you, but of the ship."

27:25. "Be of good cheer: for I believe God, that it shall be even as it was told me."

I. HISTORICAL SETTING. When Paul had come to the end of his trials with Roman governors it was decided that he should be sent to Rome. He had appealed to Caesar under his political franchise as a freeman of Rome, so this was the outcome. The rulers who had been in a dilemma saw the way out for them. On the one hand, the Jews had pressed them to condemn Paul. On the other hand, their sense of justice and knowledge of law had reminded them that Paul was entitled to a fair trial. But they were unwilling to make the decision to carry out any further trial in Caesarea. To Rome then went Paul. This was the providential way for him after the early wish was never granted in a normal way. Now he would go as under the Emperor's escort for trial.

II. EXPOSITORY MEANING. The description of the voyage to Rome is the work of an eye-witness and historian throughout and the language of a navigator. The map charts the course.

Acts 27:1. "When it was determined that we should sail." This was a decision of critical judgment.

Acts 27:10. "I perceive that this voyage will be with hurt and damage ... ship ... lives." How could a landsman tell this?

Acts 27:11. "Nevertheless the centurion believed the master

149

and the owner of the ship, more than . . . Paul." This was the natural feeling and point of view for those who were used to travel by sea.

Acts 27:15. "We let her drive [drift]."

Acts 27:20. "All hope that we should be saved was then taken away" — a dreadful situation with sense of being abandoned.

Acts 27:22. "There shall be no loss of life — but of the ship." Here was comfort in the midst of danger.

Acts 27:23. "There stood by me . . . the angel of God, whose I am and whom I serve." This statement implies the ownership and service of a slave in Roman days. Paul's relationship to his Master is realistic. He is "under orders." A messenger of God stood by him. We read here of service *(latreuō)* in a liturgical sense, doing service bit by bit, carrying out a planned way.

Acts 27:24. "Brought before Caesar." Paul wished to see Rome, and his appeal to be tried under Caesar was granted. This was God's guarantee of safety in the storm. Not only that, but "God hath given thee all them that sail with thee." This was an extra in God's gracious love and mercy.

Acts 27:25. "Be of good cheer." The second time for good cheer *(euthumeite)* — not "cheer" as cheer up, but be heartened in spirit and passion. "I believe God." Faith in God is the foundation of everything. The Christian knew what to do.

Acts 27:33. "Paul besought them all to take meat." Only Christianity is balanced and sensible. It cares for the body also.

Acts 27:34. "This is for your health." Health and holiness together make a complete man.

Acts 27:35. "He . . . gave thanks to God," *(eucharistēsen)* — a eucharistic thanks, as in the Lord's Supper. How easily the divine and natural intermingle; the spiritual and material.

III. DOCTRINAL VALUE. The voyage and its shipwreck point up the changing points of view of men and the unchanging faith of the Christian. Master and owner of the ship were bewildered; the centurion in charge of prisoners was flustered; the soldiers thought only of killing; the sailors wished to save their own lives: only Paul, the Christian had the presence of mind to make decisions. This reveals that faith in God is the one reality in time of trouble. Faith is the foundation of life and here faith triumphs.

IV. PRACTICAL AIM. When a storm rages and the shipwreck is near, then hope is abandoned generally. At that low level of life there is not much to be done except wait and see what happens. However, when men's hearts fail for fear and others think of fatalism, the Christian can stand out with faith and courage. Faith is a means of action and it implies courage in the face of adversity.

V. HOMILETICAL FORM

Theme: "Crisis and Confidence."

Introduction: The record of the shipwreck here is one of the thrilling stories of the Bible. Nowhere do we have such graphic and harrowing details told in a manner to stir the imagination and challenge our faith. Luke describes this with the skill of the master-historian. The voyage was dangerous and the passengers and crew of the ship were exhausted and fearful. Only the apostle Paul knew what to do in the crisis. The man who knew God by faith was wiser than the men who knew the sea. He is one out of three hundred people involved, yet his personal faith can change the outlook.

A. *The Crisis.*

To reread this narrative is to imagine the whistling winds, the straining ropes, the buffeting of the waves, and the ship in danger of falling to pieces. The ship was "frapped with hawsers"— undergirding — and this helped a little. After soundings for depth, they cast the four anchors, and they also lightened the ship by jettisoning some cargo. All to no purpose. At last under the darksome night, without stars or light, drifting, and all hope gone, they present a spectacle of doom and disaster. When fear and panic beset a group of people, then worse acts could follow.

Many have experienced other kinds of storms in human story. Social, political, financial, national, moral and spiritual crises have occurred from time to time. After quiet waters of progress for the race have come storms which bring upheaval and threatened shipwreck for nations and men. In international circles we are beset by these disasters in modern days. Men's minds are full of fear and fatalism in the presence of technological inventiveness and threatened atomic doom. Economic strain has proved too much in the tensions between those who have and those who have not. Crises are everywhere in our world. The sky is dark and little light shines. Storm and possible shipwreck are predicted by scientist and politician, humanist and sociologist. Only the Christian in the church of Christ can stand up with an answer.

B. *The Challenge.*

What is this voice that rings out? Who dares to offer counsel when sailors, soldiers, passengers, and masters have agreed what is best? Who dares to break in when he is not recognized as one who knows? "Cheer up!" Is that all?

(1) Is this superficial? Is this a whistling in the dark to keep up courage? Is this mockery to speak thus? When people face disaster, who dares to taunt them? No, this is not a casual cheer up: this is the language which says, "be strong in spirit and sanity with strength of purpose and heart." No need to cry "doom" when there is hope still.

(2) Is this shallow thinking? No, this is born out of experience of other dark nights in prison and trial, with proof of God's presence and deliverance. This is not sluggish thinking, but realistic optimism, neither blind nor foolish. Faith is born of conviction.

C. *The Confidence.* "I believe God."

The secret of faith lies in personal trust and confidence in Almighty God through Jesus Christ. Paul had gone through much and had been sustained constantly.

(1) "I believe." He is saying, "I have faith and I have courage: I am not afraid." Faith is a means of knowledge and a source of action. It also brings power and strength to live. The object of faith is the determining factor. Those on the ship were no doubt religious in having some superstitious

response to idols. Were Paul and Luke the only Christians on board? Then his faith was different.

(2) "God." The supreme object of faith is found in the revealer and creator, the sustainer of life, and the providential orderer of all things. Pagans without faith in God believed Paul who had such faith in God. Not by fatalism nor by fanaticism were men saved. Only by Christian faith were the people saved from that doomed ship. Against all contrary circumstances, panic, would-be murder, starvation, death — the way out came by one man's personal faith in God. To say this and to live by it in the dark night of the storm is to have the courage under test which will bring the soul through to the morning.

The Christian faith exemplified by Paul was balanced and sane. It provided for food and health; it cared for life and property in proper relationship; and it inculcated the courage which enabled men to do that extra for the testing hours. As the ship drifted and fourteen nights passed by, the sailors had given up hope. Pessimism, hunger and despair took hold of the people. Paul's faith and courage was shown by his caution when he advised them to eat. The man of faith is the man of common sense. The care of the body is included in the whole man of faith. Revolt is nipped in the bud when people are fed and satisfied usually. Communism and riots are not possible when Christianity has a chance to reach people first of all.

Paul said, "I believe God." Jesus said, "Ye believe in God, believe also in me."

Acts 28

MISSION ACCOMPLISHED

28:16. "when we came to Rome."

28:30. "And Paul dwelt two whole years in his own hired house."

28:31. "Preaching the kingdom of God, and teaching those things which concern the Lord Jesus Christ, with all confidence, no man forbidding him."

I. HISTORICAL SETTING. After the voyage and the shipwreck the party came to the island of Malta. There they remained for three months, and then took another ship which brought them to Italy. Various places are mentioned as ports of call, and then, finally, they land and were met by brethren from Puteoli. These escorted Paul on his last walk to that city. Others came out from Rome to meet him and brought Paul encouragement for the rest of the way. In Rome he was placed under protective custody and given certain freedoms. With these he was able to continue to witness for Christ to all who came to him. Thus he had come to Rome, not as he had thought in the beginning, but under escort and awaiting trial under Caesar.

II. EXPOSITORY MEANING. In the details of this last journey for Paul there are suggestions of truth to link the ordinary life with the divine plan. Travel and fellowship combine to enrich Paul's last years of ministry and bring opportunities unknown before.

Acts 28:1. "And when they had escaped." How much was behind this word. The voyage, the shipwreck, the dangers to life, and the final thrilling experiences of deliverance.

Acts 28:2. "No little kindness" *(philanthropian)*. This philanthropy from that source was surprising. Their thoughtfulness is noted in "kindling a fire ... because of the rain

154

and cold." This probably saved many of the rescued from death.

Acts 28:3. "Paul had gathered a bundle of sticks"— a human touch of concern and thought. Paul was not too removed from life to omit this simple task.

Acts 28:4, 6. "This man is a murderer . . . a god." How often this is done to the profit of all. We need the open mind, not to swing from one extreme to another, but to be ready to receive truth from any quarter. The hermetically sealed mind is dangerous.

Acts 28:13. "The south wind blew." Note the change after the storm with Euroclydon (northeast wind) (27:13, 14). This last brought Paul safely to the shores of Italy. A quiet ending and arrival after a stormy passage.

Acts 28:15. "Appii Forum . . . the Three Taverns" — a hostel for travelers and for soldiers.

Acts 28:20. "For the hope of Israel I am bound with this chain." Paul conceived the promises of the Old Testament were fulfilled in the Christ of the New Testament.

Acts 28:22. "Concerning this sect" *(anōston)* — one of the knowing groups springing up in the Empire. "Every where . . . spoken against." An anti-christian spirit can assist in the spread of truth. When a movement is attacked, people are interested to find out something about it.

Acts 28:23. "To whom he expounded and testified . . . persuading." Jewish evangelism at its best. The occasion, the subject, the methods, and the time.

Acts 28:24. "Some believed . . . and some believed not." This is true always, from our Lord's day until now — division.

Acts 28:31. "Preaching the kingdom of God"— as a herald proclaims. "Teaching those things which concern Christ"— the doctrines of the Christian faith. "With all confidence" — no one to hinder as he confidently and strongly witnessed. Matthew 28:19 had so ordered and promised.

III. DOCTRINAL VALUE. Divine providence is displayed throughout this story. God's sovereignty overrules the affairs of men. Enemies of the gospel sought to hinder and thwart, but God's plan moved on to fulfilment. Storms, imprisonments, even threat of death cannot stop the onward march of the gospel throughout the world.

IV. PRACTICAL AIM. To demonstrate the power of the Holy Spirit in the lives of God's servants. As they obey the command to evangelize and spread the gospel throughout the whole world, then God works with them for the completion of the task. Nothing can hinder the final expansion of the church as it moves out from its original center to encompass the whole world. The work of Christ continues to this day, unhindered. Success is measured by the work of the Spirit in conversions. God uses human agents for this purpose. Adversaries oppose the work, but the church under persecution is powerful as it advances through storm and trial to victory.

V. HOMILETICAL FORM
Theme: "Mission Accomplished."

Introduction: In this vivid and moving story we see how everything that happened to Paul turned out for the furtherance of the gospel. Paul had desired to see Rome, to preach there and to witness for Christ. Undoubtedly he had hoped to visit on his own and as a free man. Now he arrived as a prisoner, but his chains are honorable. He used them as an opportunity to reach others who might not have heard the gospel. God's ways are not our ways as His thoughts are above our thoughts.

A. *The Last Stage.* 28:1-15

On the way Paul encounters many people and shares many unusual experiences.

(1) Three months at Malta (28:1-10). Here we note the kindness of the barbarians. Instead of "wreckers" they proved to be friendly and kind. The paganism of Malta was better than the piety of Jerusalem for Paul. Paul's life was endangered when the viper struck him. The reptile may have been among the sticks, and Paul in his short-sighted eye condition might not have noticed. Death was expected from a bite. That Paul "shook off" this viper might mean that Luke had something to do with cauterizing the wound in

the fire? Paul had his doctor with him. This deliverance led
some of the barbarians to imagine he was a murderer first,
and then later a god. So people can change their minds!
In Acts 14:11 a similar experience had come to Paul with
Barnabas: then it was first a god, and later a man.

Paul's ministry on the island was beneficial in the healing
ministry. This was in concert with Dr. Luke, whose medical
term "healed" is *etherapeuonto*. There is no record that
Paul preached.

(2) Twelve Days travelling (28:11-15). The voyage was
resumed and the apostle was relieved to go on the way again
towards Rome. Each place on the map shows the near approach of the final destination. To get ashore again and walk
was for Paul the realization that the climax of all his journeys was near. "So we came to Rome" (28:14) carried with it
the pathos of the sufferings encountered on the way, the
delays, the trials, the threats, and the unforeseen providences.
What a story for Paul to tell when he shared this with his
friends. It is Luke who will write the story for the church.

B. *Two Years Ministry in Rome.* 28:16-31

This last summary of Paul's city ministry brings to a close
the record of the Acts.

(1) Interviewing the Jews (28:16-29). "To the Jew first"
was Paul's word when he wrote his letter to the Roman
Church. Now he contacts his own kinsmen. A summary of
this is given and a favorable impression is made. Surprising-
ly, these Jews had not heard of the charges against Paul by
the Jews of Jerusalem. Paul covered the Old Testament
writings as the basis of persuading the Jews to accept Christ
as the Messiah. Their own Scriptures brought them the truth
of the gospel, but the same Scriptures condemned them (cf.
Isaiah) when they rejected that truth. As always the results
of evangelism point to "some believe" and "some believe
not" (28:24). This has been true since our Lord began his
work and continues even now.

(2) Preaching the Gospel (28:30-31). After Jewish evangelism comes the witness to all who come to visit Paul in
his lodging under guard. Awaiting trial, he uses the time

to witness and spread the gospel. "The Kingdom of God" looms large in his message. We wish he had given more exposition of this truth. "Teaching those things which concern the Lord Jesus Christ" suggests the unfolding of the doctrines of the faith which affirm the death and resurrection and also the Lordship of Christ. "With all confidence" tells that Paul had boldness and conviction in all he did and said. "No man forbidding him" points to the fact that no human power thwarted this effort. Freedom was granted to him to speak and to write. "Openly and unhindered" he worked on to the end.

Friends ministered to him. Roman members of the church came to him. Onesimus, the runaway slave, was converted and Paul wrote his personal note to Philemon. Epaphroditus brought a gift. Luke attended to Paul's needs. Paul wrote his prison letters to Colossae, Philippi, Ephesus. Was Luke planning his writing of the Gospel and penning part of The Acts?

The ending of this book is sudden, almost abrupt. Nero is the despot on the throne and Paul is the solitary prisoner in a city dungeon. Those were the days when Rome was like other city metropolises with all its miseries, vices, and follies exaggerated and without Christ! Nero is no more, but Paul abides through the New Testament which tells his story and in the hearts of countless Christians who follow his example. The story of The Acts continues as the Lord of the church carries forward His work by the conquests of the Spirit. To look back over the history of The Acts enables us to look up with faith and to look forward with hope.

BIBLIOGRAPHY

Barclay, W., *The Acts of the Apostles* (Daily Study Bible), Edinburgh: St. Andrews Press, 1953

Blaiklock, E. M., *The Acts of the Apostles* (Tyndale New Testament Commentaries), London: Tyndale Press, 1959

Brown, C., *The Acts of the Apostles* (A Devotional Commentary), London: Religious Tract Society, n.d.

Bruce, F. F., *The Acts of the Apostles* (Greek Text), London: Tyndale Press, 1951

———, *The Acts of the Apostles* (New London Commentary on the New Testament), London: Marshall, Morgan & Scott, 1954

Cadbury, H. J., *The Book of the Acts in History*, New York: Harper & Brothers, 1955

Carter, C. W. and Earle, R., *The Acts of the Apostles* (Evangelical Commentary), Grand Rapids: Zondervan Publishing House, 1959

Debelius, M., *Studies in the Acts of the Apostles*, London: Student Christian Movement, 1956

Demaray, D. E., *The Book of Acts* (Shield Bible Study Series), Grand Rapids: Baker Book House, 1959

Dodd, C. H., *The Apostolic Preaching and its Development*, New York: Harper & Brothers, 1937

Erdman, C. R., *The Acts*, Philadelphia: Westminister Press, 1919

Ferris, T. P., *The Acts of the Apostles* (Exposition), The Interpreter's Bible, New York: Abingdon Press, 1954

Findlay, J. A., *The Acts of the Apostles*, London: Epworth Press, 1934

Henry M., *Commentary on the Holy Bible*, Grand Rapids: Baker Book House, 1960

Interpretation, A Journal of Bible and Theology, Vol. XIII, No. 2, April 1959, Richmond

Jackson-Foakes, *The Acts of the Apostles* (Moffatt New Testament Commentary), London: Hodder & Stoughton, 1931

Jackson-Foakes and Lake, Kirsopp, *The Beginnings of Christianity,* London: Macmillan Co., 1920-33

Knox, W. L., *The Acts of the Apostles,* Cambridge: University Press, 1948

Knowling, R. J., *The Acts of the Apostles* (Expositor's Greek Testament), London: Hodder & Stoughton, 1917

Lenski, R. C. H., *The Interpretation of the Acts of the Apostles,* Columbus: Wartburg Press, 1944

Lindsay, T. M., *The Acts* (Handbooks for Bible Classes) Edinburgh: T&T Clark, n.d.

Luccock, H. E., *The Acts of the Apostles in present-day preaching,* New York: Harper & Brothers, 1938

Macgregor, G. H. C., *The Acts of the Apostles* (Introduction and Exegesis), The Interpreter's Bible, New York: Abingdon Press, 1954

McLaren, A., *The Acts* (Bible Class Expositions), London: Hodder & Stoughton, 1894

————, *The Acts of the Apostles* (Exposition of Holy Scripture), London: Hodder & Stoughton, 1907

Morgan, G. C., *The Acts of the Apostles,* Westwood: Fleming H. Revell Co., 1924

Pickell, C. N., *Preaching to Meet Men's Needs,* the meaning of The Acts as a Guide for Preaching Today, New York: Exposition Press, 1958

Rackham, R. B., *The Acts of the Apostles* (Westminster Commentaries) London: Methuen & Co., 1901

Ramsay, W. M., *The Bearing of Recent Discoveries on the Trustworthiness of the New Testament,* Grand Rapids: Baker Book House, 1953

————, *Pictures of the Apostolic Church,* Grand Rapids: Baker Book House, 1959

———, *St. Paul the Traveller and the Roman Citizen,* Grand Rapids: Baker Book House, 1960

———, *The Cities of St. Paul,* Grand Rapids: Baker Book House, 1960

Robertson, A. T., *The Acts of the Apostles* (Word Pictures of the New Testament), New York: Harper & Brothers, 1931

Scroggie, W. G., *The Acts* (The Study Hour Series), London: Marshall, Morgan & Scott, 1933

Stokes, G. T., *The Acts of the Apostles* (The Expositor's Bible), London: Hodder & Stoughton, 1893

Thomas-Griffith, W. H., *The Acts of the Apostles,* Chicago: Moody Press, 1947

Turnbull, R. G., *The Promise Unto You,* Studies from The Acts, Philadelphia: Board of Christian Education, the Presbyterian Church in the U.S.A., 1948

Williams, C. S. C., *The Acts of the Apostles* (Harper's New Testament Commentaries), New York: Harper & Brothers, 1957

Williams, R. R., *The Acts of the Apostles* (Torch Bible Commentaries) London: Student Christian Movement, 1953

Others not listed include the works of John Calvin, J. P. Lange, as well as the many studies on the Life of Paul, and on the History of the Church.